CULTIVATING
Holy Beauty

BOOK 3: *Walking In the New*

This Book Belongs to:

．．．

BY JESSIE NORTH

www.CULTIVATINGHOLYBEAUTY.com

Fourth Printing May 2021

Visit *www.CultivatingHolyBeauty.com*

Contents

Acknowledgements

Father,

Thank You for sending the most important person in my life to save me, Your Son, Jesus. You never withheld your love from me. You are always willing to meet me where I am, all the while lovingly walking me into a new understanding of your heart. I can't wait to see what tomorrow holds! Jesus, I'm so thankful it's You!

Thank You, Father, for my husband, Adam—one of Your best soldiers. He loves and cares for me and our children with all he has. He is always willing to let me be me, even when it's hard. From childhood friend to life-long lover, thank You, Father, for choosing Him. Adam, I'm so glad it's you!

Thank You for our children. I praise You for blessing them with patience, faithfulness, and courageous hearts for truth, purity, and adventure. I praise You Father for blessing my life with theirs. You could have given them to anyone, but You chose me to be their mother. They are more than I deserve! Noah and Bowen, I'm so glad it's you!

Father, I thank You for the countless volunteers who helped in getting this work ready to be published! Thank you for the women who allowed me to be a part of their journey, and for sharing their stories on the pages of Cultivating Holy Beauty. Please bless them all, Father!

I love You,

Jessie

Welcome to Walking In the New

A NOTE FROM THE AUTHOR

Sisters,

You made it! Way to go—I'm rejoicing with you right now! Over the past several weeks you have learned how to get rid of the infection left behind by lies. Most of the hard work has already been done through "Letting the Healer Heal" as you learned how to pour out your heart to God, allowing Him into your hurt and anger. It's time for a little clean up now that the infection is gone! Many Christians become discouraged when they realize they have fallen back into the same cycles of sin. Healing is an ongoing process, a daily renewal of trusting in His ability to pardon and justify. In Book 3, "Walking In the New" or W.I.N. you will discover how sin is often an outward manifestation of unaddressed wounds of the heart. Now that you have begun processing the wounds of your heart, you can now more effectively identify and turn from sinful patterns that may have been caused by those wounds, Praise Him—He is so good to us!

It's time to tear off the labels from your past and embrace your identity in Christ! I encourage you to be open palmed to the Holy Spirit with your life and choices throughout this journey. The more you are willing to surrender to Him, the more freedom you will find! There will be challenges ahead as you learn to allow God to rewrite the things you once valued for the things He loves. As we fully surrender ourselves to the Spirit of God living in us—allowing Him to convict our hearts of sin—we come more into alignment with His heart and His goodness. God always gives you a choice, and He loves you the same no matter what road you choose to walk down. However, true intimacy is a choice—it can't happen without your consent. It's not forced affection behind closed doors. He waits for you—open palmed—to give to you and receive from you. Will you choose Him? Will you allow Jesus to be the King of your heart by putting away the things that keep you distant from Him and start pursuing the things that close the distance between the two of you? It may sound hard, but trust me, He will meet you every step of the way! I have found that whatever He calls you to put away, He will match it 1,000 fold! This is how we grow closer to our Lord daily—we choose to put off the old so that He can dress us in the new, every day!

When it comes to fabric, I am a texture girl. I imagine my new dress given to me by my precious Heavenly Father is much like Cinderella's ballgown in Disney's 2015 remake of "Cinderella." I know in my heart, because of Jesus, I'm no longer worthy of the rags I once wore. Every morning, I get to choose what I put on, the old rags or the new dress. I choose to remember all Jesus and I have been through together. I choose to walk in the newness of His Spirit, living in me.

Enjoy learning how to let God become your everything in "Walking In the New!" He is worth it! You are worth it!

May I be found with my Jesus,

Jessie

You Were Made for This!

GROUP LEADER NOTES

It's time to begin training members in your group to lead. At times, it seems some people are born with the confidence of a natural leader, while others may fear to step forward. *Cultivating Holy Beauty* is designed to not only help you grow spiritually but also equip you to lead others to the same truths you have learned through the study. Below are some points to help you train the next generation of disciple-makers.

- Whether or not all your group members go on to multiply is between them and God, not you. Either way, love your group members well and trust that God is in control!

- Be sure to reach out to each leader-in-training to pray with them, encourage them, and answer any questions or squelch any lies they may be hearing before it's their turn to lead. Communication is key!

- Instruct them to read through all of the sections below, leading up to Lesson 1, "Walking In the New."

- Make sure you reviewed one of the Leader's Guides with the leaders-in-training.

- During the meeting time, be confident to sit back and let them lead—yet willing to help if feel they are struggling.

- Encourage the leaders-in-training to follow the Leader's Guides.

- It's okay for the leaders-in-training to make the lesson their own, as long as they follow the Leader's Guide.

You Were Made for This!

PARTICIPANT LEADER NOTES

In Book 3, "Walking In the New" (W.I.N.), the group participants begin taking turns leading the weekly meetings to help you grow as a leader in a safe environment.

- Your group leader will assign the lessons you are to lead, walking with you through every step of the way!

- Purpose to keep open communication with your group leader about any concerns, hesitations, or worries you may have. Allow her to speak truth over you and help dispel lies you may be hearing.

- Be sure to read through all of the sections below leading up to Lesson 1, "Walking In the New."

- Your group is a safe place to learn and grow not only in your relationship with Jesus, but also as a disciple-maker!

- Follow the Leader's Guide. The Leader's Guides have been field-tested and are in place to help you stay on track.

- You may not have realized it, but God has already been using you to minister to your fellow group members through the sharing of your Quiet Times and being transparent about your journey—failures and all.

- You were made for this! Upon becoming a believer, we are commanded to go and make disciples of all nations, baptizing in the name of the Father, the Son, and the Holy Spirit and teaching them to obey the commands of Jesus (see Matthew 28:19-20). Now that you are growing and learning not only the commands of Jesus but how to obey them, it's time to begin teaching others the same!

- Begin asking God to prepare your heart to lead a group of your own someday. Don't fear! Your job is to love people well and point them to Jesus, letting the Holy Spirit do the rest!

Are you the Group Leader?

A FEW THINGS YOU NEED TO KNOW

Discussing these details up front will help you to have a successful group.

Cultivating Holy Beauty (CHB) consists of two parts:

- Part I of the *Cultivating Holy Beauty* series focuses on your vertical relationship with God and consists of three books:

    1. Book 1: Intimacy with Jesus

    2. Book 2: Letting the Healer Heal

    3. Book 3: Walking In the New or "W.I.N."

    This portion of the series may take an average of 35 weeks, not including breaks for vacations and holidays.

- Part II focuses on your identity in Jesus and your horizontal relationships such as how you view yourself, marriage, and motherhood.

- The skills taught in *Cultivating Holy Beauty* build upon one another. Be sure to complete the books in order for maximum benefit.

Group Basics

PREPARING FOR YOUR GROUP

- Welcome to "Walking In the New," the next step in your journey of growing closer to God!

- Group meeting time should still be at least two hours. More time may be needed depending on the number of people in your group. Be intentional and respectful by beginning and ending on time.

- Save extra sharing and conversation for the end. This will ensure people with obligations to husbands, children, or otherwise will be able to leave on time. Discuss the time expectations at the beginning to allow clear expectations and accountability.

- Take time to discuss if adjustments need to be made for your meeting day and time.

- Remember to set a backup day for your group to meet if someone will need to miss the regular meeting time.

- Purposing to make the meeting as stress-free as possible is key in helping your group members complete the course successfully.

- If someone needs to miss a meeting, the group leader should meet with them one-on-one, either in person or over the phone, to help them catch up.

- Discuss with your group and decide who would be comfortable leading in your absence.

- You may decide to take more than one week on certain lessons, moving at the pace of the group. True transformation is a process and cannot be rushed. However, taking longer than two weeks on a lesson can cause the group to lose momentum. Be mindful not to sit too long in one spot.

- Follow the Leader's Guide at the beginning of each lesson. It has been field-tested and will help you stay on track and lead successful groups.

- A Participant's Guide is also provided to help the group members understand how to complete the lesson.

- Pray for your group members throughout the week, being sure to keep communication flowing through texting or phone calls.

- Just as true transformation is a process, leadership is also a process. Allow yourself to grow and be cultivated as a leader.

Course Records

BOOK 3

The "Course Record" form on page 157 is there to help you stay on track. The below items are recommended before moving to the next book. The books build on one another. Please be sure to complete each book before moving to the next.

- Finish all eight lessons

- Memorize eight Scripture passages

- Record four or more Quiet Times a week

SPECIAL NOTE: Memorization may be a challenge for some. Having the verses memorized word perfect is not a prerequisite for finishing the course. Your best effort is enough!

Guidelines for A Successful Group

The following are recommended guidelines for a successful *Cultivating Holy Beauty* (CHB) group:

- Following the Leader's Guide, be sure to prioritize:

    4. Worship

    5. Pray

    6. Share Quiet Times

- Start on time. Beginning group time worshipping through music not only helps busy hearts and minds settle and focus on God, but it also helps ensure anyone running late won't miss the lesson discussion time.

- As worship comes to a close, the group leader should transition into prayer, modeling the WAR method of prayer for the group (Worship, Admit, Request).

- After the prayer time has ended, give a quick summary of the lesson from your notes written on the Leader's Guide page.

- Share Quiet Times each week following the format on page 31 of Book 1, "Intimacy with Jesus." Always encourage every member to share, although some may not be comfortable in the beginning. Continue to find ways to support and encourage participation from all members.

- In the second half of group time, continue following the Leader's Guide and be sure to:

    1. Share answers to the questions picked by the leader

    2. Discuss: Review and Before Your Next Lesson

    3. Recite memory verses

- While we want to keep the group on track, sometimes God has plans of His own that we shouldn't overthrow. There may be times when the group ministers to one particular member who is in need of having truth spoken into them and it ends up taking the whole meeting. Don't be afraid to let this happen! God is growing leaders in these moments as they minister to the hurting people around them with their new skills. It's not hard to recognize when the Holy Spirit is moving vs. someone just wanting to talk. Again, don't be afraid to let God take over.

- If time allows, discuss your highlighted questions marked on the Leader's Guide. Encourage the participants to share their answers. Often, you will find yourself being the one who speaks the least in the group because of the sharing that is taking place. This is a good sign that the Holy Spirit is doing more leading than the group leader!

- Keep the group on track. Pay attention to when the group is getting off topic. The leader should gently direct the conversation back to the study. Additional conversation can take place once the purpose for the group time has been met.

- The leader should make sure the meeting ends on the set time, being respectful of group members, family, or child care workers who may be waiting for them. If you find more time is needed for the lesson, make sure the group agrees to stay longer or use the next week's meeting time to pick up where you left off.

- Give grace to those who are experiencing unusual circumstances and need more time to complete the lesson.

- The group should be a safe place to share Quiet Times and struggles without condemnation or judgment. What is shared in the group should be kept confidential. Always ask group members before any information is shared with a spouse, pastor, or anyone else.

Addressing Hard Topics

- Discipleship is often messy. Sometimes it means you feel like you are fighting harder for someone else's walk with God than they are. This "fight" however, is done in prayer—not in person.

- Don't be afraid to share how you have struggled with sin. Be real. Being transparent glorifies the Lord when we allow people to see our failures. It highlights how good He truly is!

- As a leader, remember that you don't have to have it all figured out! Don't be afraid to let your group members minister to you when you are struggling! Be raw and real with them—it will only encourage them in their own struggles!

- If you still have a non-believer in your group, praise the Lord they have stayed this long! Keep praying for them. Don't be afraid to check in with them every so often to see how they are, and if they are ready to receive Jesus into their hearts. Don't forget this is God's plan.

- Making disciples is one of the greatest privileges we have. However, at times it can get messy, feel scary, and be at times risky. It's important to remember that God didn't give us a spirit of timidity—but of power and love (2 Timothy 1:7)! If you are feeling overwhelmed at leading a group or by a situation in your group, this may be a sign you are striving in your own strength. Take your eyes off of your group and put them back on Jesus! Your task as a *Cultivating Holy Beauty* leader is to first, continue growing in your relationship with Jesus, and second, teach others to do the same by living out your love for Jesus in front of them. As disciple makers, this is all we can do!

- *Cultivating Holy Beauty* does not authorize anyone to give professional counseling advice. This course provides skills to deeply know and love your Savior—teaching others to do the same.

- No part of *Cultivating Holy Beauty* should be used to replace professional medical care. If you feel someone is showing signs of hurting themselves or is in any danger, don't wait or second guess yourself! Reach out to your pastor, women's ministry leader or someone that you know who can offer support right away!

I Want Jesus!

A SIMPLE PLAN OF SALVATION

- If you have someone in your group who is not yet a Christian and still has not decided to receive Jesus into their hearts, keep praying for them and pointing them to Jesus at every turn! This is a precious opportunity for you to gently walk them into a beautifully intimate relationship with the Lord. God is the one in control, so rest in His plan for this group member.

- Continue not to push for them to "pray the prayer"—rejoice they are still hanging in there! There is a reason why they haven't lept yet, which will likely be uncovered soon if they allow God to show them. Don't underestimate the ways of the God of all Creation. His ways are higher—just believe He has a plan!

- Pray for them. Pray they show up each week, and that they are doing the work. If they keep coming back, trust that God is softening their heart!

- Don't be afraid to check in with them every so often to see how they are doing and if they have any questions about salvation. The most significant way to have an impact on an unbeliever is by living out your love for Jesus in front of them! Movements of God fly on the wings of testimonies! Be sensitive to the Spirit and honest with your own struggles all while letting them see that your hope comes from Jesus!

- If they come to you and want to pray to receive the Spirit of God into their heart, here are some verses to review as well as a sample prayer to lead them through. You can't mess this up—just let the Spirit lead!

WE ARE ALL SINNERS.

"For all have sinned and come short of the glory of God," (Romans 3:23 NIV).

THE PENALTY FOR SIN IS DEATH!

"For the wages of sin is death, but the gift of God is eternal life through Jesus Christ our Lord" (Romans 6:23 KJV).

GOD'S LOVE FOR US.

"For God so loved the world that he gave His one and only Son, that whosoever believes in Him shall not perish, but have eternal life" (John 3:16 NIV).

WE MUST RECEIVE HIS FREE GIFT OF SALVATION!

"If you declare with your mouth, 'Jesus is Lord,' and believe in your heart that God raised him from the dead, you will be saved. For it is with your heart that you believe and are justified, and it is with your mouth that you profess your faith and are saved" (Romans 10:9-10 NIV).

"For whosoever shall call upon the name of the Lord shall be saved" (Romans 10:13 NIV).

EXAMPLE: PRAYER OF SALVATION

Father,

I know I have missed the mark and that I am a sinner. I believe Jesus is Your Son and that He was born of a virgin. I believe He died on the cross and shed His blood to pay for my spiritual freedom. I believe He was buried and rose to life from the grave. I ask You Lord Jesus to come into my heart and make me new! Change my heart and my life Lord, I want to know You! Thank You Jesus for the forgiveness of my sins, your gift of Salvation and everlasting life, because of Your grace and mercy!

Amen.

Walking In the New (W.I.N.)

KEY POINT

Sin is a physical manifestation of heart wounds, just like the fruit of the Spirit is a physical manifestation of a life obedient to the commands of Jesus. Now that you have begun to experience healing, you must know how to continue moving towards your God-given design by not allowing hurts to take root and turn into bitterness, hardening your heart again.

WHY THIS MATTERS

Before you are anything else: wife, mother, friend, etc. you are a daughter of God. This is where the root of your affirmation must stem.

HOW TO APPLY

When you understand why a sinful pattern is in place, you are able to repent from a pure heart and turn from it—finally letting go of the old identity, and stepping into the life you were created for.

LESSON 1

Walking In the New (W.I.N.)

MEMORY VERSES

2 Corinthians 5:17 (Write your memory verse in the space below.)

QUIET TIME VERSES

2 Corinthians 5:16-21; Matthew 16:24-27; 2 Peter 1:3-4; Romans 10:1-13; Matthew 10:37-39; 2 Timothy 1:13-14; Isaiah 43:16-19

Complete Lesson 1 and try to have four to seven Quiet Times before your next meeting. To ensure you are using the verse in the correct context, be sure to read several verses before and after the suggested Quiet Time passage(s).

KEY POINT

Sin is a physical manifestation of heart wounds, just like the fruit of the Spirit is a physical manifestation of a life obedient to the commands of Jesus. Now that you have begun to experience healing, you must know how to continue moving toward your God-given design by not allowing hurts to take root and turn into bitterness, hardening your heart again.

WHY THIS MATTERS

Before you are anything else: wife, mother, friend, etc., you are a daughter of God. This is where the root of your affirmation must stem.

HOW TO APPLY

When you understand why a sinful pattern is in place, you are able to repent from a pure heart and turn from it—finally letting go of the old identity, and stepping into the life for which you were created.

Leader's Notes

- This lesson may take more than one or two weeks. If a group member has to miss, causing the group to sit longer than two weeks in a lesson, find a time to meet with her one-on-one or over the phone so the group can keep moving forward.

- Remember to be mindful to begin and end on time.

- Pray for your group as they begin to address the sinful patterns caused by the wounds Jesus revealed to their hearts in Book 2, "Letting the Healer Heal."

- Highlight one or two questions from the lesson to be discussed in group time, allowing each person to share an answer. For quick reference, write the page numbers of the questions you chose to discuss below.

Navigating Your Group Time

- Spend 15-20 minutes in worship.

- As the time of worship comes to a close, the leader should begin the WAR method of prayer.

- Write a quick summary of Lesson 1 in the space below. Share this with the group to begin the lesson after the time of prayer is finished

- Have group members share their "Main Take-Away" from the end of the lesson.

- Ask each person to share a Quiet Time.

- If time allows, ask everyone to share an answer from the questions the leader highlighted (1-2 questions).

- Read sections: "Review" and "Before Your Next Lesson".

- Break into pairs and recite your verses.

- Remind everyone to sign off on each other's course record in the back of the book.

LESSON 1

Walking In the New (W.I.N.)

MEMORY VERSES

2 Corinthians 5:17 (Write your memory verse in the space below.)

QUIET TIME VERSES

2 Corinthians 5:16-21; Matthew 16:24-27; 2 Peter 1:3-4; Romans 10:1-13; Matthew 10:37-39; 2 Timothy 1:13-14; Isaiah 43:16-19

Complete Lesson 1 and try to have four to seven Quiet Times before your next meeting. To ensure you are using the verse in the correct context, be sure to read several verses before and after the suggested Quiet Time passage(s).

KEY POINT

Sin is a physical manifestation of heart wounds, just like the fruit of the Spirit is a physical manifestation of a life obedient to the commands of Jesus. Now that you have begun to experience healing, you must know how to continue moving toward your God-given design by not allowing hurts to take root and turn into bitterness, hardening your heart again.

WHY THIS MATTERS

Before you are anything else: wife, mother, friend, etc., you are a daughter of God. This is where the root of your affirmation must stem.

HOW TO APPLY

When you understand why a sinful pattern is in place, you are able to repent from a pure heart and turn from it—finally letting go of the old identity, and stepping into the life for which you were created.

Participant's Notes

- Complete this lesson before your next meeting. Be sure to answer the questions marked with a discussion bubble and be ready to share your answers with the group. It's important to remember there are no wrong answers to the questions throughout the lessons because they are your thoughts, so be free in how you answer!

- Use the space provided in the margins to take notes, write down additional Scripture references you find, or to draw pictures that come to mind as you journey through Book 3, "Walking In the New."

- Use a concordance, lexicon, dictionary, and thesaurus as part of your Quiet Time.

- Remember to go slow and focus on the process, not the end result. True transformation is a process, not a race.

- PRAY for yourself and your other group members as you begin to address the sinful patterns caused by the wounds Jesus revealed to your heart in Book 2, "Letting the Healer Heal."

Walking In the New Life

Haley and I met through a Quiet Time class at our church where Jesus became our common ground. Haley was learning how to truly trust God with her heart for the first time in her life. She had been saved since she was a teenager, but she had never known freedom. Abandoned by her parents and abused when put into foster care, Haley's self-esteem and confidence was all but destroyed when she became an adult and entered marriage. Haley would have never known God could love her like this if she hadn't been forced to run to Him for refuge over the past few years as her marriage seemed beyond repair. Haley's past was full of hurt and betrayal, and she had begun to spiral into a deep, dark depression. She had tried all the new antidepressant medications but always felt they just masked the real problem.

Haley decided to fight for her life using the only tool that ever brought her any hope—the Word. Some days she felt like she won the battle, and others felt like a loss; but everyday Haley woke up, she faithfully suited up in the Word and tried again!

Haley's marriage had been wracked with trials from the beginning, but recently, new growth was springing up as her husband started fighting for his identity in Christ. It all came together one evening as Haley and I sat on her front porch sipping sweet tea while her husband and children played ball in the yard. God was showing Haley that He could turn even the ugliest situations into a blessing with a little faith. Haley looked at me and said, *"I realized after journaling with God the other night that I have never expected to have anything good in my life because my parents left me. I have been speaking death over myself throughout my entire life, and into my marriage. I'm past beating myself up by saying, 'I'm not good enough for my husband,' because that is not in line with what God says about me in Acts 11:9, my new Anchor Verse."* Haley quickly recited, *"Do not condemn what the LORD has called clean!"*

Warmth spread through my heart as I realized she had finally gotten it! She was finally giving control and ownership of her heart over to God! She went on to say, *"I realized I've been afraid to let go of the only way of life I have ever known. I just expected everyone to abandon and hurt me, including God."* With a bright smile, she said, *"But who am I to call a daughter of God worthless and no good!?*

It's a hard truth to walk in sometimes, but honestly, I have been adopted by my Heavenly Father! God is healing my heart, and He is showing me how to walk into my God-given design. I'm going to keep fighting for this new identity God has given me. It's been hard trying to hold on to that hope and faith when the storm rages or I begin feeling trapped in my marriage again because my husband has a bad day. I started going back to my journal and reading how far I have come with God's help, and I remember what I am fighting for! I'm thankful this is my life and these are my struggles! What a gift it is to have a choice when I wake up every morning and say, "This is a new day, and I choose You, Jesus! Day by day, hour by hour, minute by minute, second by second, and every moment in between, I choose JESUS!"

She stood up shouting with her arms raised to heaven, "I choose Jesus! I CHOOSE JESUS!" Haley's husband stopped to turn and laugh with her, as their children started running in circles singing, "I choose Jesus, I choose Jesus!" It was a beautiful moment to see the victory of Jesus in the hearts of this family that was nearly destroyed by the evil one.

Haley knew this new thought process would take some time to get used to, and there would always be a battle ahead of her; that's just life. There was a lifetime of bad habits that would take time to reprogram, but all she had to do was remember what she had become convinced of and who taught her! Haley had developed her spiritual weapons and was becoming skilled in using them. All she had to do moving forward was keep her eyes fixed on Jesus and face one day at a time, knowing God was with her.

> BY HIS DIVINE POWER, GOD HAS GIVEN US EVERYTHING WE NEED FOR LIVING A GODLY LIFE. WE HAVE RECEIVED ALL OF THIS BY COMING TO KNOW HIM, THE ONE WHO CALLED US TO HIMSELF BY MEANS OF HIS MARVELOUS GLORY AND EXCELLENCE.
> —2 PETER 1:3 NLT

Why Choosing to "W.I.N." Matters

An Internet search revealed 85% of women in an abusive relationship will return to their abuser. Can you imagine why? Sadly, the most common reason stated by the victims was, "It's what feels normal." Sometimes, all we know how to be is hurt and broken by the lies we have believed. However, that is not God's plan for you! God's way with His children is always love, joy, peace, patience, kindness, goodness, faithfulness, gentleness, and self-control. His plan is always redemption. "Walking In the New" or W.I.N. requires living by the Spirit, and boy does that take faith! Living by the Spirit is allowing God to rewrite your earthly ways for His heavenly ways. Now that you have experienced Jesus binding up your broken heart and setting you free from lies, it is time to set your sights on the road ahead.

"Walking In the New" will help you develop a battle strategy against the old way of life by identifying idols and strongholds. When wounds have been festering for a long time, it is easy to understand how they can be your "normal," some may say "comfortable," but that is not living in the freedom of Jesus Christ. Now that you have begun allowing Jesus to bind up whatever hurts you have and set you free from lies, it's time to finish the job by tearing down any strongholds that may be lingering from any bad habits connected to the old way of life. You are worth the effort this journey is going to take. If this level of trust in Jesus were easy, everyone would have it—but it's not. When you take off the old, you must put on the new by allowing God to fill that space in your heart with the knowledge of His love. If you don't fill in the space with God's love, you will end up returning to your default mode.

> **WHEN AN EVIL SPIRIT COMES OUT OF A MAN, IT GOES THROUGH ARID PLACES SEEKING REST AND DOES NOT FIND IT. THEN IT SAYS, "I WILL RETURN TO THE HOUSE I LEFT." WHEN IT ARRIVES, IT FINDS THE HOUSE SWEPT CLEAN AND PUT IN ORDER. THEN IT GOES AND TAKES SEVEN OTHER SPIRITS MORE WICKED THAN ITSELF, AND THEY GO IN AND LIVE THERE. AND THE FINAL CONDITION OF THAT MAN IS WORSE THAN THE FIRST.**
> **—LUKE 11:24-26 NIV84**

Living the New Life

COLOSSIANS 3:1-25 ESV

³ If then you have been raised with Christ, seek the things that are above, where Christ is, seated at the right hand of God. ² Set your minds on things that are above, not on things that are on earth. ³ For you have died, and your life is hidden with Christ in God. ⁴ When Christ who is your life appears, then you also will appear with him in glory.

⁵ Put to death therefore what is earthly in you: sexual immorality, impurity, passion, evil desire, and covetousness, which is idolatry. ⁶ On account of these the wrath of God is coming. ⁷ In these you too once walked, when you were living in them. ⁸ But now you must put them all away: anger, wrath, malice, slander, and obscene talk from your mouth. ⁹ Do not lie to one another, seeing that you have put off the old self with its practices ¹⁰ and have put on the new self, which is being renewed in knowledge after the image of its creator. ¹¹ Here there is not Greek and Jew, circumcised and uncircumcised, barbarian, Scythian, slave, free; but Christ is all, and in all.

¹² Put on then, as God's chosen ones, holy and beloved, compassionate hearts, kindness, humility, meekness, and patience, ¹³ bearing with one another and, if one has a complaint against another, forgiving each other; as the Lord has forgiven you, so you also must forgive. ¹⁴ And above all these put on love, which binds everything together in perfect harmony. ¹⁵ And let the peace of Christ rule in your hearts, to which indeed you were called in one body. And be thankful. ¹⁶ Let the word of Christ dwell in you richly, teaching and admonishing one another in all wisdom, singing psalms and hymns and spiritual songs, with thankfulness in your hearts to God. ¹⁷ And whatever you do, in word or deed, do everything in the name of the Lord Jesus, giving thanks to God the Father through him.

¹⁸ Wives, submit to your husbands, as is fitting in the Lord. ¹⁹ Husbands, love your wives, and do not be harsh with them. ²⁰ Children, obey your parents in everything, for this pleases the Lord. ²¹ Fathers, do not provoke your children, lest they become discouraged. ²² Bondservants, obey in everything those who are your earthly masters, not by way of eye-service, as people-pleasers, but with sincerity of heart, fearing the Lord. ²³ Whatever you do, work heartily, as for the Lord and not for men, ²⁴ knowing that from the Lord you will receive the inheritance as your reward. You are serving the Lord Christ. ²⁵ For the wrongdoer will be paid back for the wrong he has done, and there is no partiality.

TURNING TOWARD YOUR FUTURE

Two common mistakes after cleaning out your heart are 1) thinking the hard part is over and 2) not knowing where to go next. As gross as it sounds, we are like a dog returning to its vomit (Proverbs 26:11) when we don't replace the old way of life, thought process, or habit with a godly one. God's Word is the only voice that should be heard when learning how to walk in your new identity. Only God sets captives free, so be careful what you allow to replace the past. This book, "Walking In the New," is a guide to help you learn how to continue walking forward into freedom.

I like The Message's paraphrased version of Matthew 16:25:

> THEN JESUS WENT TO WORK ON HIS DISCIPLES. "ANYONE WHO INTENDS TO COME WITH ME HAS TO LET ME LEAD. YOU'RE NOT IN THE DRIVER'S SEAT; I AM. DON'T RUN FROM SUFFERING; EMBRACE IT. FOLLOW ME, AND I'LL SHOW YOU HOW. SELF-HELP IS NO HELP AT ALL. SELF-SACRIFICE IS THE WAY, MY WAY, TO FINDING YOURSELF, YOUR TRUE SELF. WHAT KIND OF DEAL IS IT TO GET EVERYTHING YOU WANT BUT LOSE YOURSELF? WHAT COULD YOU EVER TRADE YOUR SOUL FOR?
> —MATTHEW 16:25 MSG

I believe this is what Jesus was talking about when He said, "and anyone who does not take up his cross and follow Me is not worthy of Me. Whoever finds their life will lose it, and whoever loses their life for My sake will find it" (Matthew 10:38-39 NIV). When we purpose to keep turning away from the old way of life that held us in bondage, no matter how long it takes, we lose our identity in the world and find our true selves in Jesus. He promises that if we take on this challenge of yanking up our personal battles by their heavy roots, and carry them to Him, then through Him we will find freedom. What a beautiful promise!

Taking up your cross and carrying it is all about trusting Jesus with the hard stuff—the stuff you don't want to hold on to, but you also can't seem to let go of. By purposing a vertical mindset, of keeping your focus on Jesus and His way, over a horizontal mindset of searching for approval from people and consolation in material things, you actually start to get somewhere.

> **SO FROM NOW ON WE REGARD NO ONE FROM A WORLDLY POINT OF VIEW. THOUGH WE ONCE REGARDED CHRIST IN THIS WAY, WE DO SO NO LONGER. THEREFORE, IF ANYONE IS IN CHRIST, HE IS A NEW CREATION; THE OLD HAS GONE, THE NEW HAS COME! ALL THIS IS FROM GOD . . .**
> **—2 CORINTHIANS 5:16-18A NIV84**

FREEDOM TAKES FAITH!

Even though it is hard, God has given you the strength you need to live each day in freedom—to turn away from the old ways of life. Sometimes, claiming truth will be a moment-by-moment choice. The temptation to give into lies from the old way of thinking and hopelessness will try to creep in slowly or waylay you in the moment! This is when remembering *and* putting into practice everything you've learned so far will be vital for maintaining the progress you have made (2 Timothy 3:14 NIV).

IF FAITH WAS EASY, EVERYONE WOULD HAVE IT.

You are now a woman of the Word—you know Truth! Through *Letting the Healer Heal*, you have grown in your faith. Now as you continue allowing Jesus into your deep, hurt places, your sword is being sharpened and continues to be honed as you memorize and meditate on God's Word and His character. This is your greatest defense! Knowing the Truth is the only way to defeat a lie. Don't forget: from the moment you were born, Satan has been fighting for your soul through lies, temptation, and distraction. The enemy is passionate about stealing, killing and destroying any and everything that God loves—including, and especially, you! When you asked Jesus to be the Lord of your life, you stepped onto the spiritual battlefield. As you continue to grow closer to God, the battle will escalate! Don't sheath your sword, sister! It is time to move into a defensive position—which is bowed low in prayer—this is how we fight out battles!

The enemy is preparing a strategy to take back the ground in your heart that he recently lost. Do not sit down to celebrate your victory; there will be time for that in heaven! While you are here on Earth, you are in enemy territory. You cannot afford to let down your guard, lest you be taken captive again!

YOUR SPIRITUAL WEAPONS

Throughout this book, "Walking In the New," or "W.I.N" you will become very familiar with what God says is needed to walk successfully in the new for a lifetime, putting more distance between you and past behavior. Everything you've learned up to this point, including how to have a Quiet Time, meditating on Scripture, memorizing Scripture, the WAR method of prayer, writing Hurt Letters to God, flipping lies, and my favorite, hearing Love Letters from God, are all vital weapons in your growing arsenal against the enemy. The goal is for you to finish this battle on earth as a whole and healthy daughter of God. A daughter fit for battle and confident in her weapons because she knows whose strength is wielding them—her heavenly Father!

Remember, as you move forward, always keep your gaze fixed on Jesus! The enemy will tempt you, bait you, set you up, and try to knock your feet out from under you. Have faith, warrior sister of mine! You are not being tempted by anything that is uncommon to humankind (1 Corinthians 10:13)! Hold your ground and keep doing what is right. Be a woman who believes the Word is her ultimate battle strategy!

DON'T BE AFRAID; JUST BELIEVE.
—MARK 9:23B NIV84

Do you believe " Walking In the New" can be as simple as making a choice every day to seek God and His will for your day?

What is your favorite spiritual weapon you have learned since beginning the journey of *Cultivating Holy Beauty* (How to have a Quiet Time, meditating on Scripture, memorizing Scripture, the WAR method of prayer, writing Hurt Letters to God, flipping lies, hearing Love Letters from God)? Explain your answer:

How have the skills you've learned from the other lessons equipped you for this new way of life?

Take some time and think this through. Letting go of the old and walking in new life means you will need to let parts of yourself go—elements that aren't good for you. Are you ready to do that? What might you gain through letting go?

Review

1. Now that you have experienced healing, you must know how to continue moving toward your God-given design by not allowing hurts to take root and turn into bitterness, hardening your heart again.

2. Always keep your gaze fixed on Jesus.

3. Everything you've learned up to this point—how to have a Quiet Time, meditating on Scripture, memorizing Scripture, the WAR method of prayer, writing Hurt Letters to God, flipping lies, and hearing Love Letters from God—are all vital weapons in your growing arsenal against the enemy.

Main Take-Away

What was your main take-away from this lesson?

Before Your Next Meeting

1. Try to have a Quiet Time at least four times this week using the verses listed for Lesson 2.

2. Memorize **Romans 5:1-2** this week.

Notes

Justified

KEY POINT

The blood of Jesus is your worth—you are priceless!

WHY THIS MATTERS

When you believe in your heart that Jesus is enough, you stop trying to find your value in the world.

HOW TO APPLY

Remember what you have become convinced of and who taught it to you. When you start believing the blood of Jesus is your worth, you begin to live life by the Spirit!

LESSON 2

Justified

MEMORY VERSES

Romans 5:1-2 (Write your memory verse in the space below.)

QUIET TIME VERSES

Romans 5:1-8; Romans 14:5-23; Colossians 2:1-15; Hebrews 6:4-6; Romans 3:21-27; Galatians 2:17-3:9; Ephesians 2:8-10

Complete Lesson 2 and try to have four to seven Quiet Times before your next meeting. To ensure you are using the verse in the correct context, be sure to read several verses before and after the suggested Quiet Time passage(s).

KEY POINT

The blood of Jesus is your worth—you are priceless!

WHY THIS MATTERS

When you believe in your heart that Jesus is enough, you stop trying to find your value in the world.

HOW TO APPLY

Remember what you have become convinced of and who taught it to you. When you start believing the blood of Jesus is your worth, you begin to live life by the Spirit!

Leader's Notes

- This lesson may take more than one or two weeks. If a group member has to miss causing the group to sit longer than two weeks in a lesson, find a time to meet with her one-on-one or over the phone so the group can keep moving forward.

- PRAY for your group as they learn about their true value in Christ!

- The group leader should highlight two or three questions from the lesson to be discussed in group time. Have each person share an answer.

- Highlight one or two questions from the lesson to be discussed in group time, allowing each person to share an answer. For quick reference, write the page numbers of the questions you chose to discuss below.

Navigating Your Group Time

- Spend 15-20 minutes in worship.

- As the time of worship comes to a close, the leader should begin the WAR method of prayer.

- Write a quick summary of Lesson 2 in the space below. Share this with the group to begin the lesson after the time of prayer is finished

- Have group members share their "Main Take-Away" from the end of the lesson.

- Have each person share a Quiet Time.

- If time allows, have each person share an answer from the questions the leader highlighted (1-2 questions).

- Read sections: "Review" and "Before Your Next Lesson".

- Break into pairs and recite your verses.

- Remind everyone to sign off on each other's course record in the back of the book.

LESSON 2

Justified

MEMORY VERSES

Romans 5:1-2 (Write your memory verse in the space below.)

QUIET TIME VERSES

Romans 5:1-8; Romans 14:5-23; Colossians 2:1-15; Hebrews 6:4-6; Romans 3:21-27; Galatians 2:17-3:9; Ephesians 2:8-10

Complete Lesson 2 and try to have four to seven Quiet Times before your next meeting. To ensure you are using the verse in the correct context, be sure to read several verses before and after the suggested Quiet Time passage(s).

KEY POINT

The blood of Jesus is your worth—you are priceless!

WHY THIS MATTERS

When you believe in your heart that Jesus is enough, you stop trying to find your value in the world.

HOW TO APPLY

Remember what you have become convinced of and who taught it to you. When you start believing the blood of Jesus is your worth, you begin to live life by the Spirit!

Participant's Notes

- This lesson may take two weeks to complete. Understanding your worth is justified by the cross and is very important. Be sure to take your time through this lesson.

- Use a concordance, lexicon, dictionary, and thesaurus to go deeper in your Quiet Time.

- PRAY for your the members of your group to truly grasp the reality of their worth. No one can take it away or diminish it.

- Use the space provided in the margins to take notes, write down additional Scripture references you find, or to draw pictures that come to mind as you journey through "Justified"

Justified

Father,
I love You, and I love the way You love me. I love that I can be all You created me to be—that You created safe boundaries for me to dance in . . . be free in . . . be me in. I was made to worship You—I was made to love You and be loved by You. I am okay with being different, Lord. I am okay with not taking justice into my own hands when I feel misunderstood, disrespected, or unappreciated. Thank You for creating me to love You this way.

Help me cast the rest of my cares upon You. Show me how; lead me, and I will follow. I believe Your dreams and visions, I believe when Your voice speaks, and I love how Your Word guides me and Your Spirit pursues me. You are the best accountability partner I could ask for! You are always with me, and You still have my best interest at heart.

Father show me how to be increasingly more sensitive to You, to see people less and You more. I'm crying out to You, Father. I want to know You and be known by You! Freezing cold darts up into my veins and I shudder at the thought of hearing You say, "Depart from Me. I never knew you!" Help me open all the doors I have closed off to You in my heart that cause unbelief! There will be no shut doors to You, Lord of my life! I am not ashamed of my love for You; I am not ashamed of You Jesus! Know me, search me—let me sing at the top of my lungs for You in praise and fall to the floor in worship. I'll be a fool for You, not careful for You. I'm over it; I'm over myself! I give all of me to You, over and over again. I'm not loving You carefully and safely anymore . . . no, not ever again! You are my worth! You are all I have!

Forgive me for trying to justify my worth and value with other things and people! Forgive me for allowing the cares and traditions of man to take Your place in my heart. God, I have continuously allowed the concerns and opinions of others to determine my value and limit my love for You. It stops here! Set alarm bells in me, Lord! And when I get close to this place again, set them off like a fire alarm! Let the desires of my flesh burn to the ground, God—this is my sin to which I keep returning. Help me stop, Father!

You have called me to be holy and set apart. I will seek Your face day and night. You are my worth and my strength—You are my Hero . . . Jesus . . . only Jesus.

Purge my heart of all that offends You—that which rejects what You did on the Cross for me. I will seek You more. Open doors for me to walk through that will lead me deeper into Your heart. Hide me there. Hold me there. When I fall short, when my feelings get hurt—I will turn to You for my worth. When I am treated unjustly, I will step back and let You be my Defender. You clear my name. You say, "Not guilty," even when I have done nothing to earn Your Name written on my heart. The lies try to take me, the darkness tries to claim me, yet You say, "She is MINE!" They flee, and I am saved. I search the room for the familiar gaze to settle my anxiety, looking and looking. Finally, I see You—our eyes lock. My eyes fill with the gaze of my Love . . . my Savior . . . my Hero. Your peace and knowing flood me. I am safe. I am found.

I don't have all the answers, but You do. I don't know the whole Truth, but You do. I don't see the way out, but You do. I don't know the meaning, but You do. I can't overcome the lie, but You can. I can't win the battle, but You will. I can't defeat the enemy, but You have. You are more than enough for me. Your Son is more than enough for me. Your Spirit is more than enough for me. I'll drink the cup You have poured for me. I'll stand in the gap You made for me.

With all my love, Father,
Jessie

"He who hears not the music,
thinks the dancer is mad."
—Anonymous

FOR WE HOLD THAT ONE IS JUSTIFIED BY FAITH
APART FROM WORKS OF THE LAW.
—ROMANS 3:28 ESV

Justification by faith is so important to grasp because it is what sets Christianity apart from all other belief systems. No other religion serves the God of Creation who was willing to send His only begotten Son to die in our place. All other religions and even some labeled as "Christian" say you have to work your way to God. If that were true, then it nullifies what Jesus did on the Cross, making His suffering and sacrifice pointless. Nothing God does is pointless or wasted! For many of you that sounds obvious, but what about the areas deep in your heart, where you believe who you truly are is not enough for God?

There are places like that in all of us to some degree. These lies drive you to try to earn your worth through perfection of home and hearth, acts of service from an empty cup, success in academia, career, ministry, or other achievements, and so on. What happens when those things are stripped away from you, and all you are left with is the vessel you came in? Are you worthless because you have nothing to offer? What happens when, no matter how hard you try, you can't measure up to the world's standards of beauty? Does that mean you are unlovable? NO.

In the space below write the words: MY BELIEF IN JESUS JUSTIFIES ME!

Abraham

I love the story of Abraham. It's such a beautiful picture of God's confidence as our Defender. It gives me such hope as a daughter with so many questions inside! When you find yourself thinking, "Who am I to be used by God?" remember Abraham! Abraham was an unknown man whom God called out of his country and away from his family. He was of the Chaldeans who were referred to as "astrologers" or "pagans" because they worshipped the heavens rather than the One who created them. God promised Abraham that if he would leave his father's pagan household and go where He showed him, God would make him into a great nation and bless him. He would even bless those who blessed Abraham and curse those who cursed him (Genesis 12:1-3)! Talk about being vindicated!

DON'T LOOK TO OTHERS FOR VALIDATION, ONLY JESUS CAN JUSTIFY YOUR WORTH.

When others, like the Egyptians and Pharaoh tried to hurt or take Abraham's wife Sarah, God inflicted a severe disease on them because they meant to harm Abraham (Genesis 12:11-20). This is our God being faithful to His promise! Abraham was not a young man when God called him; he was 75 years old! And not only that, it's not like Abraham's dad was a pastor—no, Terah worshipped the moon! This is who God called to be the father of faith—a seemingly nobody! When he left his homeland, headed to the land God was calling him to. God had him camp in corrupt cities whose inhabitants hated God. Here, Abraham was to build altars for the LORD and call on His name . . . amidst the pagans . . . in their city!

When I look at Abraham's story, I am amazed: His family worshipped things other than God. At the age he was called, most people nowadays have long since retired. He had no children. However, God was giving him promises about his offspring that were to come. Moreover, because he believed what he had heard from the LORD, it was credited to him as righteousness!

My favorite part is the more profound message of how Abraham talked with the LORD about Him sparing any righteous people that may have been in Sodom. It wasn't what I would call a "typical" conversation, and to my mind, it seemed risky. This story shows how Abraham believed in God's love for him, and how he was able to talk to the Father as a son, confident that God would listen and consider what he had to say.

This realization changed how I began to approach my Heavenly Father's lap. Instead of being afraid of rejection, I found myself running to Him, filled with joy, expectation, and careless abandon because of His goodness and love for me. God obviously cared about Abraham's thoughts because in Genesis 18:17 it says, "the LORD contemplated telling Abraham about destroying Sodom and Gomorrah." Picture Abraham sitting in the opening of his tent, where the LORD had just appeared to Him. Abraham proceeded to ask God a series of "what ifs" to which God not only entertained but also agreed.

FAITH IS A GIFT— BELIEF IS A CHOICE.

Toward the end of the conversation, I guess Abraham started to feel like the child who was on the verge of asking one too many questions, when he said, "Please don't be angry, but let me just ask one more question." The Father replied in agreement with Abraham. Abraham was so convinced of God's love and promise that he didn't fear to ask God to reconsider His plan. Not once, but six times, Abraham asked boldly of the LORD. God did find righteous people in Sodom (see also 2 Peter 2:7). The Father, neither threatened nor worried by what Lot's daughters would later do, spared them from the destruction of the town for Abraham's sake because he stood in the gap for his righteous nephew, Lot.

Does this give you a better grasp of the type of relationship we are called to with the Father? It does for me! Through the recount of Abraham's walk with God, we are called to greater faith, as we are children of Abraham. Let us have faith and believe God, walking and talking with Him as Abraham did, and it will be credited to us as righteousness.

ROMANS 4:18-25 NIV84

[18]Against all hope, Abraham in hope believed and so became the father of many nations, just as it had been said to him, "so shall your offspring be." [19]Without weakening in his faith, he faced the fact that his body was as good as dead—since he was about a hundred years old—and that Sarah's womb was also dead. [20] Yet he did not waver through unbelief regarding the promise of God, but was strengthened in his faith and gave glory to God, [21] being fully persuaded that God had the power to do what he had promised. This is why "it was credited to him as righteousness." [23] The words "it was credited to him" were written not for him alone, [24] but are also for us, to whom God will credit righteousness—for us who believe in him who raised Jesus our Lord from the dead. [25] He was delivered over to death for our sins and was raised to life for our justification."

A HURT LETTER FROM A SISTER IN CHRIST . . .

Father,
This morning I believe it takes more faith to believe God loves you if you are a woman than it does if you are a man. My suffering is nothing compared to the suffering of Jesus, but Father, my heart is hurting. I wait with earnest expectation to see if I made the cut as a woman. What will your verdict be when I stand before you at the end of my life? Was I quiet enough in church, yet did I make my mark in the world? Was I sexy enough for my husband, yet soft enough for my children? Did I measure up? What a sad thing for me to say! I'm so confused! I hear You say, "you are Mine, and I am yours, I am your worth, and I am your value," yet I get waylaid by the opinions of others.

Father, You know my heart, so there is a lot I don't have to write out to state my case. In the moment, I wait for Your words to come to me, to justify my worth, to shut down the accusation from the world, but You are silent. I wait in my weakness and silence, vulnerable and angry, hot tears roll down my cheeks—wanting to be justified in front of all who judge and persecute me with their looks and thoughts.

All I get is silence. Somehow, my mouth stays closed, and I do not sin in my anger . . . in my hurt I do not give in to the temptation of the enemy to argue and prove my point . . .

*I continue to wait for You. I'm embarrassed and filled with shame over my emotions as I run to my secret place where we have our long conversations, where so many of our memories have been made. In my inner-room I have hung pictures as reminders of our time together—the truths You have taught me. The walls shimmer and sparkle with Your written Word. I find You there, as I always do, waiting for me with open arms. "Well done," You say, as You soothe me and stroke my hair while I sob into Your lap. "I did it again," I cry, "I tried to find my worth in the world . . . when will I ever learn? Father, it hurts so much!" You continue to hold me, and say, "But You ran to **Me** this time . . . I am your worth . . . I am your value." You let me find my way to the Truth You have taught me. You are patient and gentle with me, holding and not scolding me. I get it now Lord; You are my worth, Father! Truly . . . deeply . . . through and through. I am Yours alone. You are the Potter, and I am Your clay. Your peace floods me; I am home in Your arms. I am safe.*

I am priceless to the God of Creation. My role is different, but I am no less valuable than my brothers in Christ—sons and daughters—all children of the King. Help me see the warning signs when I am trying to find my home in the world, when the only address I have is in Your Kingdom, Father. You are my value! You are my worth! I will stop trying to give it away. Thank You, Lord, my precious Father, thank You.

SINCE WE HAVE BEEN JUSTIFIED THROUGH FAITH, WE HAVE PEACE WITH GOD THROUGH OUR LORD JESUS CHRIST . . .
—ROMANS 5:1 NIV

These are the battles—like yielding to a godly husband when you don't feel like he deserves it but choosing to do so anyway because you love Jesus more than you love your pride. This is when you know your heart is in alignment with the Father because you desire justice for what Jesus did on the cross more than you want justice for yourself. Your successes or failures do not measure your worth. To the extent you believe in Jesus is the extent that you're able to grasp how important you are to the Father! Your worth is measured by your belief in Jesus. Nothing and no one on earth is your salvation, only Jesus. That is something no one can take from you. Successful or failed marriages are not your worth. Successful or wayward children are not your worth.

Sanctification is being conformed to the image of Jesus through His Word and Spirit. Often, the most growth will come through trials and suffering. However, know this: God wastes nothing and will use the hard situations of life, even the ones you bring about, to sanctify you as you continue to go to His Word and wrestle through. Justification by faith is the foundation for BELIEVING you are loved by God because of what Jesus did on the cross.

Let me encourage you to be so rooted in the Word and confident in who you are in Christ, that no matter the circumstances around you, it doesn't change your character and how you react. Justify your actions based on the Cross of Jesus Christ and not by the behavior of those around you! There is nothing you can do to prove yourself worthy to the world because the standards are always being raised—yet all the while being lowered.

Jesus' offering on the cross is your worth! Nothing compares to this! When I think I know what's best for myself and charge ahead taking justice into my own hands, instead of keeping Jesus' commands at the forefront, I am claiming to know what's best for me. Therefore, I end up making myself foolish and giving my pride the victory rather than Jesus.

When I seek honor for myself before the honor of God, I exchange the glory of the incorruptible God into an image made like the corruptible man. I become my own God. Life becomes about my desires, my happiness, my joy, my justice and my comfort—what pleases me and not God. When I take justice into my own hands, attempting to justify myself, I will always fall short because God will not share His glory with another. However, when I choose to honor the commands of Jesus in the middle of my battles because I trust that He will defend me, I have been justified by faith.

Are you willing to let God rewrite your value system?

If so, how might you stick to this new plan when life gets hard or when your desire is different from God's desire?

How will you know if your desire is different from God's desire?

What skills have you learned that will help you discern God's desire?

Review

1. When you choose to value what Jesus values, you prove your love to Him.

2. Purpose to keep fighting for Truth until it becomes your new reality!

3. The work of the cross makes you "enough."

4. Your circumstance doesn't change the truth of the cross or the power of the blood!

Main Take-away

What was your main take-away from this lesson?

Before Your Next Meeting

1. Try to have a Quiet Time at least four times this week using the verses listed for Lesson 3.

2. Come prepared having finished Lesson 3.

3. Memorize **Galatians 1:10** this week.

Notes

Surrendered

KEY POINT

One of the hardest things about learning how to yield to the Lord is understanding what it looks like in certain situations. Yielding to God never means being a doormat but being a doorway—not a stumbling block, but a stepping stone—for Him to work through you! This lesson teaches how to choose God in hard times instead of pushing forward in our own strength.

WHY THIS MATTERS

Choosing self-control by allowing Jesus to be your worth when you feel offended and hurt by other's can turn a hopeless situation into a hope-filled opportunity to share Jesus.

HOW TO APPLY

When you learn how to choose God's way over your own, and not walk in your won strength—especially when it hurts—you experience freedom in Christ!

LESSON 3

Surrendered

MEMORY VERSES

Galatians 1:10 (Write your memory verse in the space below.)

QUIET TIME VERSES

Galatians 1:6-10; Luke 21:34-36; Romans 8:5-17; 1 Corinthians 15:33; 1 Thessalonians 5:15-18; Amos 5:14; 1 Corinthians 9:24-27

Complete Lesson 3 and try to have four to seven Quiet Times before your next meeting. To ensure you are using the verse in the correct context, be sure to read several verses before and after the suggested Quiet Time passage(s).

KEY POINT

One of the hardest things about learning how to yield to the Lord is understanding what it looks like in certain situations. Yielding to God never means being a doormat but being a doorway—not a stumbling block, but a stepping stone—for Him to work through you! This lesson teaches how to choose God in hard times instead of pushing forward in our own strength.

WHY THIS MATTERS

You can turn a hopeless situation into a hope-filled opportunity to share Jesus, by choosing self-control and allowing Him to be your worth when you feel offended.

HOW TO APPLY

When you learn how to choose God's way over your own, and not walk in your own strength—especially when it hurts—you experience freedom in Christ!

Leader's Notes

- This lesson may take more than one or two weeks. If a group member has to miss causing the group to sit longer than two weeks in a lesson, find a time to meet with her one-on-one or over the phone so the group can keep moving forward.

- PRAY for your group as they find freedom in being a woman under God's control!

- Encourage the group to keep pouring their hearts out to God through Hurt Letters since new hurts can happen every day, as well as allowing God to speak His love to them through Love Letters.

- Highlight one or two questions from the lesson to be discussed in group time, allowing each person to share an answer. For quick reference, write the page numbers of the questions you chose to discuss below.

Navigating Your Group Time

- Spend 15-20 minutes in worship.

- As the time of worship comes to a close, the leader should begin the WAR method of prayer.

- Write a quick summary of Lesson 3 in the space below. Share this with the group to begin the lesson after the time of prayer is finished

- Have group members share their "Main Take-Away" from the end of the lesson.

- Have each person share a Quiet Time.

- If time allows have each person share an answer from the questions the leader highlighted (1-2 questions).

- Read sections: "Review" and "Before Your Next Lesson".

- Break into pairs and recite your verses.

- Remind everyone to sign off on each other's course record in the back of the book.

LESSON 3

Surrendered

MEMORY VERSES

Galatians 1:10 (Write your memory verse in the space below.)

QUIET TIME VERSES

Galatians 1:6-10; Luke 21:34-36; Romans 8:5-17; 1 Corinthians 15:33; 1 Thessalonians 5:15-18; Amos 5:14; 1 Corinthians 9:24-27

Complete Lesson 3 and try to have four to seven Quiet Times before your next meeting. To ensure you are using the verse in the correct context, be sure to read several verses before and after the suggested Quiet Time passage(s).

KEY POINT

One of the hardest things about learning how to yield to the Lord is understanding what it looks like in certain situations. Yielding to God never means being a doormat but being a doorway—not a stumbling block, but a stepping stone—for Him to work through you! This lesson teaches how to choose God in hard times instead of pushing forward in our own strength.

WHY THIS MATTERS

You can turn a hopeless situation into a hope-filled opportunity to share Jesus, by choosing self-control and allowing Him to be your worth when you feel offended.

HOW TO APPLY

When you learn how to choose God's way over your own, and not walk in your own strength—especially when it hurts—you experience freedom in Christ!

Participant's Notes

- Complete this lesson before your next meeting. Be sure to answer the questions marked with a discussion bubble ⬤ and be ready to share your answers with the group. It's important to remember there are no wrong answers to the questions throughout the lessons because they are your thoughts, so be free in how you answer!

- Use a concordance, lexicon, dictionary, and thesaurus to go deeper in your Quiet Time.

- Keep pouring your heart out to God through Hurt Letters, since new hurts can happen every day, as well as allowing God to speak His love to you through Love Letters.

- PRAY for yourself and your fellow group members as they find freedom in being a woman under God's control!

- Use the space provided in the margins to take notes, write down additional Scripture references you find, or to draw pictures that come to mind as you prepare to have a "Surrendered" heart before the Father.

A Woman Under God's Control

A letter from a woman who is dear to my heart; but God's love for her far surpasses my own.

Hi Jessie!

I think insecurity is something that we all struggle with as females. Everyone has their own insecurities that plague them, whether it be looks, singleness, money, job security, affirmation or awards, childlessness, people pleasing, envy, materialism, and so forth. The list can go on and on. I know this, yet it is hard not to live in the flesh (see Galatians 5:19).

You and I were discussing if romance novels are considered porn. We decided to apply some questions of discernment to it: Does it draw me closer to God or push me farther away? Does it cause me to sin? Does it cause me to desire someone in a sexual way that is not my husband? Does it cause me to desire something I don't have in an impure way? As I sit here and struggle with my issues, it is not ironic to me that this is where our conversation led. I think we all have our secret sins, and so I am finally going to get mine out and not let it be a secret any longer. I know that we need to share our sins with each other (see James 5:16), which may be one of the hardest things God asks us to do. For a while now, I have known and have been convicted that I needed to confess my sins not only to God but also to a fellow believer. However, who wants to tell your darkest, ugliest secrets to anyone in case they see you differently? Well, apparently now is my time.

Again, you didn't know this has been one of my biggest issues when we started talking about being a woman under God's control the other day. I may not have physically had sex with anyone, but mentally I have, and is that not the same thing to God (see Matthew 5:27-30)? If you look at someone lustfully, then reading and lusting is the same as looking. With the novels also comes masturbation, which is a dirty word that no one talks about. I know that mentally imagining you are sleeping with someone is a sin because I am not guarding my heart against lust (see Romans 7:23; Philippians 3:19). It feels good, so it can become an addiction.

Regretfully, this is something I have struggled with for years, but over the past year I have come to see it for what it is and can't justify it anymore. Sex is meant for two people to come together as one (see 1 Corinthians 6:16; Ephesians 5:31).

I will have to talk to my future husband about it one day, and that makes me sad and scared. You are supposed to guard your mind and master your physical desires. This all goes back to insecurity. When I am feeling the most lonely and "woe is my singleness" is when it becomes the hardest to say no to that desire. Instead of turning to God, I turn inward, relying on myself to feel better. I then beat myself up for it later, feeling like a dirty loser.

I have had to throw my books away . . . well, I'm in the process of it . . . and deleting them from my iBooks. I do not need that temptation. Admitting that I had a problem was hard. It is so easy to rationalize and pretend otherwise. A verse that has caught my attention and made me choke when I read it is Song of Songs 2:7 and 3:5 which say, "Do not arouse or awaken love until the time is right."

I don't want to taint my imagination with the world's interpretation of what intimacy between a man and woman should look like. These novels can give warped and unrealistic views of what it means to be in a relationship, and certainly, of what godly men are really like! I found myself being attracted to men like the ones described in the romance novels instead of men who were chasing after God. I want God's view of marriage and what intimacy between a husband and wife should look like. I want my mind to be purified!

I need to have control of my mind, fantasies, and daydreams. Our minds are a dangerous place when we are not pursuing a relationship with God. Jesus is enough for me, whether I ever get married or not! Until then, I will worship God and cherish my singleness.

Thank you for giving me this opportunity to share and to confess. I love you, and may God lead and guide you throughout this writing process!
In Christ,
Marley

SELF-CONTROL

While I may not have struggled with the same things as my friend, I do know the struggle with self-control. I became frustrated at how quickly I seemed to return to my old ways when things were tough and stress was high. I would revert to my old default mode of taking matters into my own hands to curb whatever desire was ruling me at the moment. I thought about the very first woman, Eve. What was her problem? No, really—what was her big downfall? I mean, she was in the garden! How could she have failed so miserably and completely? Over the years, I heard many opinions about Eve and the fall. Most dripped with disgust and contempt.

I, however, was not of that camp. I wanted to apply the skills I had learned through my Quiet Times to the passages about Eve and ask God to analyze my heart with His truth. I had not figured out how to get through a whole day without turning my back on God in some way, and it was starting to infuriate me.

This was when I began my quest to learn how to become a woman under God's control and not my own. One of the most effective tools I use to understand the meaning of Scripture is to look up the verse in many different translations. I appreciate how the paraphrased "Message" version of 1 Corinthians 9:27 helped me see there is constant work to be done to ensure it is the Spirit I am being led by, not my desire for a comfortable life here on earth.

I DON'T KNOW ABOUT YOU, BUT I'M RUNNING HARD FOR THE FINISH LINE. I'M GIVING IT EVERYTHING I'VE GOT. NO SLOPPY LIVING FOR ME! I'M STAYING ALERT AND IN TOP CONDITION. I'M NOT GOING TO GET CAUGHT NAPPING, TELLING EVERYONE ELSE ALL ABOUT IT AND THEN MISSING OUT MYSELF.
—1 CORINTHIANS 9:27 MSG

Look up 1 Corinthians 9:27 in a variety of translations. Write out the version that speaks to your heart the most in the space provided below.

Back to the Beginning

THE FIRST WOMAN . . .

I started reading at the beginning—verse one, chapter one, book one—Genesis. I found a piece of my identity as a woman in the very first chapter, where God painted this beautiful picture for me of how He made "woman" in His image (see Genesis 1:26-27). Immediately, I knew I had gone to the right place for Truth. I read through the creation of woman and was reminded of the careful and creative beauty of my design (see Genesis 2:20-25).

When I entered into chapter three of Genesis though, I stopped in my tracks at what God revealed to me. The revelation was, without question, how I saw my daily actions mirrored in Eve's. As I read through the text, God showed me step by step how her fall happened and how I do the same thing almost daily!

The Fall

GENESIS 3:1-6 NIV

Now the serpent was more crafty than any of the wild animals the Lord God had made. He said to the woman, "Did God really say, 'You must not eat from any tree in the garden'?"

2 The woman said to the serpent, "We may eat fruit from the trees in the garden, 3 but God did say, 'You must not eat fruit from the tree that is in the middle of the garden, and you must not touch it, or you will die.'"

4 "You will not certainly die," the serpent said to the woman. 5 "For God knows that when you eat from it your eyes will be opened, and you will be like God, knowing good and evil."

6 When the woman saw that the fruit of the tree was good for food and pleasing to the eye, and also desirable for gaining wisdom, she took some and ate it. She also gave some to her husband, who was with her, and he ate it.

FIXING OUR EYES ON GOD

The first thing I noticed was Eve was not confident of the words God had spoken—she was not a woman of the Word which made her prime real estate for the enemy. The enemy said, "Did God really say . . . ?" Soon Eve became confused, leaving the door open for the enemy's one-two punch of idolatry and lack of self-control. He first hit by striking her God-given appreciation for beautiful and functional things, but twisting it by weaving sickly idolatry in with deception: "*When the woman saw that the fruit of the tree was good for food and pleasing to the eye, and also desirable for gaining wisdom . . .*" The second blow was her lack of self-control. After Eve gave in to the blind adoration of the banned fruit, she lacked the self-control to stop herself, taking it from the enemy and eating. Sadly, it doesn't stop there. She had one last safe barrier in place that she chose to ignore. I found myself wondering where Adam was all this time. I wondered if he had been off tending the garden or something? As my eyes finished reading the verse, my heart sank into the pit of my stomach as I read, "*She also gave some to her husband, who was there with her, and he ate it.*"

"Aw, Eve!!" I thought. God gave her plenty of opportunities to get out of this! What might have happened if she had turned to Adam and said, "Babe, do you think this is a good idea? What was it God said about the fruit from this particular tree?" I'm not saying that would have stopped the progression of the fall, but it is highly possible. Eve failed to seek godly counsel in the face of her battle. I know when I allowed a voice of reason into one of my "make or break" moments, I have experienced sin come to a halt in its tracks as God used the wise counsel of another who spoke spiritual wisdom into me.

LET US LEARN FROM EVE— CHOOSE TO TALK TO THE FATHER— NOT A SNAKE!

However, **Eve's overarching error was that she engaged in battle with the enemy, and the enemy deceived her.** *She stepped forward, right out of her design, taking her eyes off God, and joined in a deadly debate with an intelligent liar. Eve held her ground for about one round before he out-intellectualized her. All the while, she only had to cry out to her heavenly Father for help, and He would have defended His precious creation.*

LET US LEARN FROM EVE

We will never win a battle by taking our eyes off of God!

1. We must be women of the Word, or we will fall into deception. There are consequences for us not knowing the truth, and the result is sin, which separates us from our Maker!

2. We must not put anything—family, career, hobbies, trials, education, relationships, fears, and so on—ahead of God. When we do, these become our idols.

3. We must learn to use self-control!

4. When we find ourselves confused and unsure of the right choice, reach out and seek godly counsel.

5. Most importantly, keep your eyes on Jesus. Above all else, call out to your heavenly Father, and do not engage the enemy on your own. Eve walked with God in the garden. I believe she was closer to Him than you or I will get to experience this side of Heaven, and yet she barely made it one round with Satan. Don't be fooled into thinking you are better than Eve! Call on the Name of Jesus, your great Defender!

Pride

DID GOD REALLY SAY . . .
—GENESIS 3:1 NIV84

Can you see that walking in your own strength and relying on yourself is the root of pride? When you say, "I've got this God; my way is better," you are ultimately telling God you don't need His commands or the sacrifice of His Son. Pride says, "My strength is just as good as God's strength." It plants seeds of self-reliance and thinking your way is better. This is not keeping the commands of Jesus. When you don't follow the commands of Jesus, you don't prove your love for Him (see John 14:15), and you get hurt.

What might have happened if Eve had chosen to talk to the Father instead of a snake?

Do you have moments where you hear the snake whisper, "Did God really say?"

In what area of your life is self-reliance an issue?

I recommend writing to God about these areas. Think back to the Heart Illustration from "*Letting The Healer Heal.*" Sin can be an outward expression of an inner problem. To walk cancer-free, you must first be healed of the cancer. Cutting out the "tumor" so to speak, doesn't ensure that what caused the tumor has been healed and that it won't return later—much like sin, when we haven't gotten to the root issue of what's causing it. Before you can expect results of turning away from these issues of pride, you must first allow God to reveal the cause of it. Write any notes or thoughts God brought to your mind.

Reputation vs. Relationship

One of the hardest parts of allowing God to rewrite your heart with His way is choosing to value His ways over your own. Loving God will require you to make hard choices and turn away from certain things you enjoy. It may even cost you the reputation you built among your friends. Just as God convicted my friend in the story above about her lack of self-control, the Holy Spirit is continually searching your heart, trying to reveal the places that are out of balance.

Are you willing to listen? I assure you of this: If what is found in your heart is godly, it won't fade but will only get stronger as you value your relationship with Him first!

YOU THINK ABOUT THE THINGS YOU LIKE.
YOU VALUE THE THINGS YOU LOVE.
YOU MAKE ROOM FOR THE THINGS YOU WORSHIP.

When I began trying to become the kind of worshipper the Lord was seeking, I asked Him to show me how. He told me I couldn't worship what I didn't love and I couldn't love someone I didn't know. Ouch!

Read the three sentences above and think about the things that you make room for in your life. What consumes most of your thoughts?

Does work stretch past "work hours?" Do children rule your every waking minute? Do you purpose God in these hard situations?

How might you bring that more into balance?

Is God glorified through your answers above? If so, how?

Glitter from the Dust

There is not a more beautiful creation on earth than a woman confident in her worth to God. When you know this in your heart, your worship enters into the purest form possible on earth. You are finally able to worship in Spirit and in Truth.

When your shield of faith is raised firmly into position, and the sword of the Spirit is lifted high, there is no room for doubt and insecurity. You become a warrior for the Most High King, the King of your heart. Rise, warrior, and find your place on the battlefield! Know the Truth and stand firm in it. Choose your battles wisely, because you know the enemy's schemes. Know when to retreat and when to fight. Allow God to teach you and hone your skills through your relationship with Him. Be willing to believe what He speaks to you, and remember your Heavenly Father NEVER breaks His promise. The days are growing short and dark. It is time to raise the shield of faith. Be ready.

YOU CAN'T FREELY LOVE SOMEONE YOU DON'T TRUST. MOREOVER, YOU CAN'T TRULY WORSHIP GOD, IF YOU DON'T KNOW HOW HE FIRST LOVES YOU.

Father,

As soon as I started to trip, You intensified Your gaze—Your stare recaptured my attention, and you steadied my feet. You flooded me with strength, and I remembered my promise to You. You reinforced my mission. This is not easy, God! This is hard, Father, and I'm okay with it! I'm okay with You being my all—my everything—who I run to, talk to, and cry to. I dare not let any person or thing fill Your place. They clamor and paw at me, Father! Let them shred my clothes—even the skin from my bones. May my gaze be so fixed on you that I reject fear and choose faith. Betrayal, rejection, judgment, and criticism from Your disciples and friends—how did you do it, Jesus? I am not You, but I want to be like You. Especially when I'm misunderstood, betrayed, rejected, judged, and condemned. My heart is for Your heart. My path looks lonely to everyone else, but they don't see what I see; they don't hear the song I'm singing. They don't see the angels playing—they don't see You! Refine me, Lord, like gold in the fire. Purify me! I don't even know what I am asking, but if it means being closer to You, then do it! Equip me with all I need to stand in front of You and hear, "Well done, My good and faithful servant!" Break off my branches that don't bear Your fruit. My life is Yours to do what You will.

Your daughter,
Jessie

Look back over your answers from the questions throughout this lesson. What parts of your life do you need to surrender to God? In the space provided, write your prayer of repentance and ask God to strengthen you in these areas.

Review

1. Choose your battles wisely, because you know the enemy's schemes. Know when to yield and when to fight. Always keep your eyes fixed on Jesus!

2. You can't fully love someone you don't trust, and you won't freely worship God if you don't know how He loves you.

3. Loving God will require you to make hard choices and turn away from certain things you enjoy (Matthew 7:13-20).

4. Eve's overarching error was that she engaged in battle with the enemy, and the enemy deceived her. Always keep your eyes fixed on Jesus!

Main Take-Away

What was your main take-away from this lesson?

Before Your Next Meeting

1. Try to have a Quiet Time at least four times this week using the verses listed for Lesson 4.

2. Memorize **Romans 12:2** this week.

Notes

Choosing What You Value

KEY POINT

Being willing to exchange old broken habits for new godly ones, only comes when we value God above all else.

WHY THIS MATTERS

When we choose the path of Jesus, instead of the world, we experience peace and satisfaction. (Matthew 5:6)

HOW TO APPLY

Learning to value what God values helps us make the right choices in life.

LESSON 4

Choosing What You Value

MEMORY VERSES

Romans 12:2 (Write your memory verse in the space below.)

QUIET TIME VERSES

Romans 12:2; Exodus 14:13-14; Galatians 5:13-26; Amos 5:14-15; Romans 1:21-32; John 14:20-21; Isaiah 1:11-19

Complete Lesson 4 and try to have four to seven Quiet Times before your next meeting. To ensure you are using the verse in the correct context, be sure to read several verses before and after the suggested Quiet Time passage(s).

KEY POINT

Being willing to exchange old broken habits for new godly ones only comes when we value God above all else.

WHY THIS MATTERS

When we choose the path of Jesus, instead of the world, we experience peace and satisfaction. (Matthew 5:6)

HOW TO APPLY

Learning to value what God values helps us make the right choices in life.

Leader's Notes

- This lesson may take more than one or two weeks. If a group member has to miss causing the group to sit longer than two weeks in a lesson, find a time to meet with her one-on-one or over the phone so the group can keep moving forward.

- PRAY for your group to begin allowing God to rewrite their value system. Be faithful to encourage them; they will need your prayer covering!

- Highlight one or two questions from the lesson to be discussed in group time, allowing each person to share an answer. For quick reference, write the page numbers of the questions you chose to discuss below.

Navigating Your Group Time

- Spend 15-20 minutes in worship.

- As the time of worship comes to a close, the leader should begin the WAR method of prayer.

- Write a quick summary of Lesson 4 in the space below. Share this with the group to begin the lesson after the time of prayer is finished

- Have group members share their "Main Take-Away" from the end of the lesson.

- Have each person share a Quiet Time.

- If time allows, have each person share an answer from the questions the leader highlighted (1-2 questions).

- Read sections: "Review" and "Before Your Next Lesson".

- Break into pairs and recite your verses.

- Remind everyone to sign off on each other's course record in the back of the book.

LESSON 4

Choosing What You Value

MEMORY VERSES

Romans 12:2 (Write your memory verse in the space below.)

QUIET TIME VERSES

Romans 12:2; Exodus 14:13-14; Galatians 5:13-26; Amos 5:14-15; Romans 1:21-32; John 14:20-21; Isaiah 1:11-19

Complete Lesson 4 and try to have four to seven Quiet Times before your next meeting. To ensure you are using the verse in the correct context, be sure to read several verses before and after the suggested Quiet Time passage(s).

KEY POINT

Being willing to exchange old broken habits for new godly ones only comes when we value God above all else.

WHY THIS MATTERS

When we choose the path of Jesus, instead of the world, we experience peace and satisfaction. (Matthew 5:6)

HOW TO APPLY

Learning to value what God values helps us make the right choices in life.

Participant's Notes

- Ask God to rewrite your value system, showing you through His Word is of true value.

- Complete this lesson before your next meeting. Be sure to answer the questions marked with a discussion bubble ⬭ and be ready to share your answers with the group. It's important to remember there are no wrong answers to the questions throughout the lessons because they are your thoughts, so be free in how you answer!

- Use the space provided in the margins to take notes, write down additional Scripture references you find, or draw pictures that come to mind as begin practicing "Choosing What You Value."

- Use a concordance, lexicon, dictionary, and thesaurus to go deeper in your Quiet Time.

Choosing What You Value

Celeste and her husband Dave had been married for eleven years before she learned how to lose an argument. It didn't seem to matter that most of the arguments were over something petty. Celeste would allow hurtful things to fly out of her mouth to prove her point. She couldn't stand the feeling of injustice in her marriage, and she wanted to prove herself capable of holding her own in an argument. After all, if she lost, what did that say about her?! On occasion, however, a stubborn lid on a pickle jar would remind Celeste that she couldn't do it all by herself. As Celeste journeyed through *Cultivating Holy Beauty*, she began learning of her worth and value to Jesus. She felt as if the Quiet Times and Scripture memory had been a "spiritual detox" for her, affecting everything around her.

As Celeste came into spiritual health and alignment with Jesus, she began to heal inside and out. She loved that God's design of woman was purposeful and thoughtful. He did not create woman to be incapable or less than her male counterpart. Instead, He created them equal and yet different. Celeste was delighting in the truth she didn't have to prove herself to God because He loved her! She was learning through Scripture that every detail of her being was deliberate. Learning how Jesus was her worth and she had been made in the image of God was so healing for her.

Life had been hard on Celeste, and she constantly felt underestimated and unappreciated by men, beginning with her father. This, however, was not how her Heavenly Father saw her. Celeste couldn't believe the freedom she had found in the Bible, of all places! She had been raised thinking God was overbearing and His Bible was a big fat rulebook of things not to do. Oh, how terribly wrong she had been! God's truth was building a new foundation of confidence in her heart. The need to justify herself was lessening as she realized how much she hated arguing. She didn't know any other way to stand up for herself when she felt slighted over an injustice.

Dave was a good husband, but sometimes she thought he was selfish and inconsiderate, causing an overwhelming need inside her to take action and retaliate out of hurt. She knew that vengeance belonged to God, but until recently, she had not been taking God's Word so seriously.

Celeste had been convicted in one of her Quiet Times to slow down and listen to God before responding in all situations, especially when hurt was involved. Since childhood, Celeste had worked overtime to prove she was worthy of others' attention, always going above and beyond what was asked of her, often pushing past her limits. However, as she learned more about her legitimate identity in Christ, she wanted to really grasp that it was her faith in Jesus that justified her worth and nothing else. No matter how much Celeste tried to prove herself to others in the past, it never resulted in her feeling more valued. Whether winning someone's approval or winning an argument, there was something that was consistently missing along with the price that was paid.

Celeste invariably felt sad and distant from Dave when they argued, whether she won the point or not. As she learned what God's presence felt like through her Quiet Times, Hurt Letters, and Love Letters, Celeste was starting to sense the distance between herself and God—especially after going for the kill shot in arguments with Dave. Every time she crossed the line from trying to help Dave understand her point of view, to willing to prove her point at any cost, it seemed His heavenly presence became distant. It was as if to say, "Check the condition of your heart, daughter." She had begun to pray and ask God to help her know when she was headed off His course.

Celeste wanted to make better choices! Ugh—this was so hard! How would she ever be able to control herself in the heat of the moment when she felt less-than? Celeste's desire to please God was beginning to become more and more important to her, and nothing seemed worse to her now than feeling apart from Him. Celeste wanted God more than she wanted retribution for her wounded heart and sometimes wounded pride.

One afternoon, Dave and Celeste started to argue over something ridiculous again. Both feeling slighted by the other, the rise in their tempers was evident in the volume of their voices. In her mind, Celeste began to cry out to God, knowing she was entering into a place where she so often lost self-control. Her desire for victory in the arguments had shifted. She only wanted God to be the victor now. "Father, help me!" she thought. "I don't want to do this! I don't want to sin in my anger! Please help me control myself!"

Without realizing it, Celeste's prayer began to pour out of her mouth in the middle of their argument. "Father, please come into this moment. I choose You, Father; I choose what is right! I choose to yield to You, Father. I choose a new way, and I am turning from the old way that only leads to hurt in my marriage. I don't want to win anymore, Father; it's not worth it. It doesn't ever prove anything anyway! Forgive me for being offended and allowing my hurt to hurt my husband. Father, take Your place as head of this marriage, as Lord of my heart! Take over! I surrender my hurt feelings to You of feeling misunderstood. Save us from each other Lord! Come into this moment; I welcome You! Take over, Lord! Please! I trust You!"

Suddenly, everything went silent. Celeste could feel the heated breaths of her husband's anger on her face, but he was no longer yelling. The moment seemed to stretch. She waited with her eyes closed to see what would happen next.

Spent, Dave collapsed onto the bench at the foot of their bed, letting his head sink into his hands. Standing still and thanking God for stopping the argument, Celeste continued to wait in silence. Dave began to pray out loud as well, "Father forgive me for speaking harshly to my wife and acting in a way that made her feel the need to defend herself to me. Father, heal us, please. Teach me how to be the husband You designed me to be. I want to love this woman well. I need Your love, Father. Thank You for the work You are doing in Celeste's heart, Lord. Please do the same in mine. She called out to You, Father, and You came!" With a soft chuckle, he said, "she *actually* yielded to You!"

Celeste and Dave both laughed now, knowing how strong-willed she was! They exchanged forgiveness as they held one another in one of the sweetest moments Celeste could remember. They had learned a new way to fight—by surrendering to each other and letting God win. This quiet little truth changed their marriage—all because they decided to yield to one another out of their love for God—and lose arguments!

What Truly Matters

As a child of God with free will, you get to choose what you value! God has equipped you with His Holy Spirit and the Word—everything you need to make the right choices and turn from the bondage of the world. Neither should be valued over the other. The Word without the Spirit is like a lamp without oil, and the Spirit without the Word is like oil with no vessel to hold it. It is the Holy Spirit that translates the spiritual truths in Scripture to your heart in a way that you can comprehend and then put them into practice. This is why ANYONE who has accepted Jesus Christ as their Savior can read the Bible and be transformed by it.

Understanding the balance of Spirit and Truth is where your new value system must begin! Next is remembering that, when you seek honor for yourself before the honor of God, you exchange the glory of the incorruptible God into an image made like corruptible man. You become your own god. Life becomes about your desires, your happiness, your joy, your justice, your comfort—what pleases you, not God.

When this becomes standard practice in your heart, it's like a snowball effect that leads to unrighteousness (see Romans 1:21-29). When you choose to take justice into your own hands and try to justify your worth through any other means than Jesus, this is justification by self or strength, which leads to utter and complete failure. When you choose to honor the commands of Jesus in the middle of your battles, because you allow Jesus to be your Defender—your worth, this is Justification by Faith. One is very right, and one is very wrong. Make sure you learn the difference and how to choose correctly.

TAKE A MOMENT TO STUDY THE *CHOOSING WHAT I VALUE* ILLUSTRATION ON THE NEXT PAGE.

. . . WISDOM IS PROVED RIGHT BY HER ACTIONS.
—MATTHEW 11:19 NIV84

Scenarios like Celeste's will be your hardest battles to fight! Celeste chose to lay her "rights" down—force aside her desire for justice by her own hands and yielding to what God desired of her. These are the battles we face every day, and the battle strategy you choose determines how much God can move on your behalf.

Example: If I start yelling and cussing at my husband because I chose hurt, over healing, unrighteousness over right and wise thinking and speaking, then in that moment it's as if I'm holding the Holy Spirit at a distance—not allowing Him to guide me through the hurt I feel. However, when I choose to yield and let my faith in Jesus be my defender—my worth—instead of trying to make it happen myself, the situation becomes an opportunity for God to be glorified.

As I bare my heart, full of truth and shrouded in love and forgiveness to my husband, my shield of faith rises, and Jesus saves me from myself once again. You

Choosing What I Value

When I get offended,
I HAVE A CHOICE
in how I respond. I can:

Tell everyone about it.

OR

Go *straight* to God in prayer.

The people I tell begin to think less of my offender.

He listens to me and gives me His (better) perspective, helping me see truth and move toward forgiveness.

They join me in speaking negatively about my offender, creating feelings of angst and ill will.

I feel peace and deep contentment. The "need" to vent to others is gone.

I have succeeded in:

- Sinning and causing others to sin;
- creating division in relationships;
- making myself more upset by re-hashing the details over and over;
- Directly, knowingly, and willfully disobeying God's Word by reacting according to my flesh rather than submitting to the Spirit.

I have honored God by choosing to surrender my will and hurt feelings to Him. He then blesses my heart with His peace, and I am able to forgive my offender.

ILLUSTRATION 3.1

cannot control how others behave, but by choosing to yield to the Spirit instead of the flesh, you can always control how you respond.

I PRAY THAT OUT OF HIS GLORIOUS RICHES HE MAY STRENGTHEN YOU WITH POWER THROUGH HIS SPIRIT IN YOUR INNER BEING, SO THAT CHRIST MAY DWELL IN YOUR HEARTS THROUGH FAITH.
—EPHESIANS 3:16-17 NIV

Always remember, the Fruit of the Spirit is your weapon against the spiritual principalities of darkness. Women of God, we are suiting up for war. Pay attention as you continue to learn the battle strategy. The battlefield is your heart, as you learned in Book 2, "Letting the Healer Heal." What you allow in, is what comes out to those around you. This is why God says, to "guard your heart above all else" (Proverbs 4:23).

The enemy is not your husband, not even your ex-husband, not your boss, your mother-in-law, your neighbor, or the rude person in the grocery store check-out line. Remember what you've learned about your foe—Satan—and Who taught it to you—Jesus! Remember too, it's love that covers a multitude of sin, not war.

FOR OUR STRUGGLE IS NOT AGAINST FLESH AND BLOOD, BUT AGAINST THE RULERS, AGAINST THE AUTHORITIES, AGAINST THE POWERS OF THIS DARK WORLD AND AGAINST THE SPIRITUAL FORCES OF EVIL IN THE HEAVENLY REALMS. THEREFORE PUT ON THE FULL ARMOR OF GOD, SO THAT WHEN THE DAY OF EVIL COMES, YOU MAY BE ABLE TO STAND YOUR GROUND, AND AFTER YOU HAVE DONE EVERYTHING, TO STAND.
—EPHESIANS 6:12-13 NIV

Will God help you in tough situations if you aren't willing to listen to Him? Explain your answer.

Is God glorified when we say, "I will show respect to my husband when he loves me better" or " I will show respect to someone when they show me respect"?

The Woman at Bethany

LUKE 7:36-50 NIV

36 When one of the Pharisees invited Jesus to have dinner with him, he went to the Pharisee's house and reclined at the table. 37 A woman in that town who lived a sinful life learned that Jesus was eating at the Pharisee's house, so she came there with an alabaster jar of perfume. 38 As she stood behind him at his feet weeping, she began to wet his feet with her tears. Then she wiped them with her hair, kissed them and poured perfume on them.

39 When the Pharisee who had invited him saw this, he said to himself, "If this man were a prophet, he would know who is touching him and what kind of woman she is—that she is a sinner."

40 Jesus answered him, "Simon, I have something to tell you."

"Tell me, teacher," he said.

41 "Two people owed money to a certain moneylender. One owed him five hundred denarii, and the other fifty. 42 Neither of them had the money to pay him back, so he forgave the debts of both. Now which of them will love him more?"

43 Simon replied, "I suppose the one who had the bigger debt forgiven."

"You have judged correctly," Jesus said.

44 Then he turned toward the woman and said to Simon, "Do you see this woman? I came into your house. You did not give me any water for my feet, but she wet my feet with her tears and wiped them with her hair. 45 You did not give me a kiss, but

this woman, from the time I entered, has not stopped kissing my feet. [46] You did not put oil on my head, but she has poured perfume on my feet. [47] Therefore, I tell you, her many sins have been forgiven—as her great love has shown. But whoever has been forgiven little loves little."

[48] Then Jesus said to her, "Your sins are forgiven."

[49] The other guests began to say among themselves, "Who is this who even forgives sins?"

[50] Jesus said to the woman, "Your faith has saved you; go in peace."

MOVED BY COMPASSION

I love how Jesus made sure the Pharisee knew the sinful woman of Bethany, whom they were disgusted by, would be remembered in His gospel because of her choice (see Matthew 26:13)! Her sins were many, but Jesus was moved to compassion for her because of how she poured herself out before him, unashamed of her raw devotion to Him in front of "high class" people. She traded in her worldly value for her divine inheritance, as Jesus was soon to trade His life for hers on the cross. I love the last sentence of this account in Luke when Jesus tells the woman it was her faith that saved her. From the faith that had been given to her, she chose to believe Jesus.

The beautiful truth here is that Jesus died for the Pharisee just as much as He died for those who loved Him. This kind of love is incomprehensible, but this is how the Father loves us. He sent Jesus to be the sacrifice for you, me, and the woman at Bethany!

Yielding to a husband, when you feel he doesn't deserve it or hasn't earned it, is like Jesus dying for people who didn't care. Being patient with children and choosing to train them instead of yell at them is like Jesus saying, "Father, forgive them, for they do not know what they do" (Luke 23:34 NKJV). These comparisons may sound extreme, but they not only help put things into perspective, but they also provide the best opportunities to live out your faith in Jesus. This is obeying the commands of Jesus!

Values

WHAT DO YOUR ACTIONS SAY?

Your actions reflect your values, and your values reflect your heart condition. Most often the thing you spend most of your time thinking about is what you end up doing. This can indicate where you may be trying to find your worth and value. Now that you are learning how much God loves you, it's time to evaluate the things you have given your time to and see if some changes need to be made.

An idol is anything in your life that you put ahead of God—yes, anything. If I serve my children ahead of God, who wins? No one—my children lose, because I am trying to pour into them from an empty cup. When I give more to my job than I do God, what happens? I get overwhelmed and burned out because I am doing my job in my own strength. When I put ministry ahead of my relationship with God, I end up ministering from my own strength, experience, and knowledge, and no one grows spiritually or gets set free. They grow closer to me, which is **not** the goal!

It is imperative to understand that by putting time with God ahead of everything else, you are ensuring everything else will fall into place. I love this comment by Martin Luther: "I have so much to do that I shall spend the first three hours in prayer."

When you are spending daily time with God in conversation and His Word, you are continually growing and being stretched. This allows God to reveal things in your life that aren't healthy for you, and because the spirit and body are connected, your health—physically, mentally, and spiritually begin to improve. "There is no health in my bones because of my sin" (Psalm 38:3b ESV).

WHOEVER HAS MY COMMANDS AND KEEPS THEM IS THE
ONE WHO LOVES ME. THE ONE WHO LOVES ME WILL
BE LOVED BY MY FATHER, AND I TOO WILL LOVE
THEM AND SHOW MYSELF TO THEM.
—JOHN 14:21 NIV

Let this verse drive you. When you choose to value what Jesus values, you show your love to Him. I yearn to know God deeper and to be known by Him. Choosing this value system means you must continuously allow the Word to cultivate your heart. The cultivation process NEVER stops while you are here on earth. Jesus's commands are the Word. To keep them, you must know them inside and out and allow the Holy Spirit to convict you of sin, including pride, idolatry, and self-reliance.

Have you ever considered that it matters to Jesus if you love Him? Ponder this for a while and then write down your thoughts (see Matthew 22:36-38, John 14:21).

Jesus wanted the sinful woman of Luke 7:36-50 to love Him because it would bring her freedom. He wants you to love Him as well. What does the above question say about your worth?

According to John 14:21, how does Jesus want us to express our love for Him?

How does this affect your heart toward Scripture memory?

BUILDING A NEW VALUE SYSTEM

When I asked a friend of mine the question above, "Have you ever considered that it matters to Jesus if you love Him?" She replied, "No actually, I haven't. I think it matters if you love Him, but I'm just a girl who continues to make mistakes." "Right," I replied, "me too, but that doesn't change the truth." I then suggested she read Luke 7:36-50 and answer the question again.

My friend had one of those "Aha!" moments. She replied, "That is such a beautiful way to see John 14:21! When I live out Jesus's commands, I prove my love for Him, which is what He wants! It also comes with the most valuable privilege—when I love Jesus, the Father loves me and Jesus reveals Himself to me!" My friend had gotten this pivotal part of the First and Greatest Commandment! It does matter to Jesus if you love Him. When you love Jesus, it should show. You begin to live sacrificially, putting aside the values of the world and your desires for earthly things, and adopting His values and desires for heavenly things.

Life by the Spirit

GALATIANS 5:16-23 NIV84

16 So I say, live by the spirit, and you will not gratify the desires of the sinful nature. 17 For the sinful nature desires what is contrary to the spirit, and the spirit what is contrary to the sinful nature. They are in conflict with each other so that you do not do what you want. 18 But if you are led by the spirit, you are not under the law.

19 The acts of the sinful nature are obvious: sexual immorality, impurity, and debauchery; 20 idolatry and witchcraft; hatred, discord, jealousy, fits of rage, selfish ambition, dissensions, factions, 21 and envy; drunkenness, orgies, and the like. I warn you, as I did before, that those who live like this will not inherit the kingdom of God. 22 But the fruit of the spirit is love, joy, peace, patience, kindness, goodness, faithfulness, 23 gentleness, and self-control. Against such things, there is no law.

GOD'S VALUE SYSTEM

Galatians 5, Ephesians 4 and 5, and Romans 8 explain everything you need to know about how to move forward in purifying your spirit by keeping the commands of Jesus. Just because you have been saved and may have experienced healing and freedom, it does not mean you won't have a daily choice to make in how you live. Your sinful nature doesn't just go away when you start purposing the things of God, but it will lessen and be easier to control as you mature. It is time to wake up, be aware, and choose a new value system based on Scripture—God's value system. Keep fighting for Truth until it becomes your new reality!

 ## Review

1. When you choose to value what Jesus values, you show your love to Him—which is what He desires.

2. Keep fighting for Truth until it becomes your new reality!

3. When you choose to honor the commands of Jesus in the middle of your battles, because you believe Jesus is your Defender—your worth, this is Justification by Faith.

 ## Main Take-Away

What was your main take-away from this lesson?

 ## Before Your Next Meeting

1. Try to have a Quiet Time at least four times this week using the verses listed for Lesson 5.

2. Come prepared having finished Lesson 5.

3. Memorize **Ephesians 4:1-3** this week.

Notes

My Everything

KEY POINT

The things you focus on is what you make room for in your life (see James 1:23-25 NKJV). How to identify the things you have put ahead of God.

WHY THIS MATTERS

Walking in greater intimacy with God causes you to walk in greater freedom in the world.

HOW TO APPLY

Focus all your being on God. Turn away from the things that led you away (see Matthew 22:37).

LESSON 5

My Everything

MEMORY VERSES

Ephesians 4:1-3 (Write your memory verse in the space below.)

QUIET TIME VERSES

Ephesians 4:1-6; Psalm 91; Galatians 4:8-11; John 3:22-30; Galatians 6:14-16; Hebrews 12:1-13; Luke 9:18-26; Romans 8:1-17

Complete Lesson 5 and try to have four to seven Quiet Times before your next meeting. To ensure you are using the verse in the correct context, be sure to read several verses before and after the suggested Quiet Time passage(s).

KEY POINT

The things you focus on are the things you make room for in your life. It is vital to identify and reprioritize anything you have put ahead of God.

WHY THIS MATTERS

Walking in greater intimacy with God causes you to walk with greater freedom in the world.

HOW TO APPLY

Focus all of your being on God. Turn away from the things that lead you away (see Matthew 22:37).

Leader's Notes

- This lesson may take two weeks to complete. Remember to be mindful to begin and end on time.

- PRAY for your group to allow Jesus to be their EVERYTHING as they learn to prioritize Jesus and His commands.

- Highlight one or two questions from the lesson to be discussed in group time, allowing each person to share an answer. For quick reference, write the page numbers of the questions you chose to discuss below.

Navigating Your Group Time

- Spend 15-20 minutes in worship.

- As the time of worship comes to a close, the leader should begin the WAR method of prayer.

- Write a quick summary of Lesson 5 in the space below. Share this with the group to begin the lesson after the time of prayer is finished

- Have group members share their "Main Take-Away" from the end of the lesson.

- Have each person share a Quiet Time.

- If time allows, have each person share an answer from the questions the leader highlighted (1-2 questions).

- Read sections: "Review" and "Before Your Next Lesson".

- Break into pairs and recite your verses.

- Remind everyone to sign off on each other's course record in the back of the book.

LESSON 5

My Everything

MEMORY VERSES

Ephesians 4:1-3 (Write your memory verse in the space below.)

QUIET TIME VERSES

Ephesians 4:1-6; Psalm 91; Galatians 4:8-11; John 3:22-30; Galatians 6:14-16; Hebrews 12:1-13; Luke 9:18-26; Romans 8:1-17

Complete Lesson 5 and try to have four to seven Quiet Times before your next meeting. To ensure you are using the verse in the correct context, be sure to read several verses before and after the suggested Quiet Time passage(s).

KEY POINT

The things you focus on are the things you make room for in your life. It is vital to identify and reprioritize anything you have put ahead of God.

WHY THIS MATTERS

Walking in greater intimacy with God causes you to walk with greater freedom in the world.

HOW TO APPLY

Focus all of your being on God. Turn away from the things that lead you away (see Matthew 22:37).

Participant's Notes

- PRAY for help in allowing Jesus to be your EVERYTHING as you learn to prioritize Jesus and His commands.

- Complete this lesson before your next meeting. Be sure to answer the questions marked with a discussion bubble ⬭ and be ready to share your answers with the group. It's important to remember there are no wrong answers to the questions throughout the lessons because they are your thoughts, so be free in how you answer!

- Use a concordance, lexicon, dictionary, and thesaurus to go deeper in your Quiet Time.

- Use the space provided in the margins to take notes, write down additional Scripture references you find, or to draw pictures that come to mind as you learn how to let Jesus be the King of your heart in "My Everything."

Cleaning House

One morning as Tamara sat down to have her Quiet Time, she came across Galatians 1:6-10 MEV:

"I MARVEL THAT YOU ARE TURNING AWAY SO SOON FROM HIM WHO CALLED YOU IN THE GRACE OF CHRIST TO A DIFFERENT GOSPEL, WHICH IS NOT A GOSPEL. BUT THERE ARE SOME WHO TROUBLE YOU AND WOULD PERVERT THE GOSPEL OF CHRIST. ALTHOUGH IF WE OR AN ANGEL FROM ABOVE PREACH ANY OTHER GOSPEL TO YOU THAN THE ONE WE HAVE PREACHED TO YOU, LET HIM BE ACCURSED. AS WE SAID BEFORE, SO I SAY NOW AGAIN: IF ANYONE PREACHES ANY OTHER GOSPEL TO YOU THAN THE ONE YOU HAVE RECEIVED, LET HIM BE ACCURSED. FOR AM I NOW SEEKING THE APPROVAL OF MEN OR OF GOD? OR AM I TRYING TO PLEASE MEN? FOR IF I WERE STILL TRYING TO PLEASE MEN, I WOULD NOT BE THE SERVANT OF CHRIST."

Tamara sat stunned for a moment, letting the meaning of the words she had just written on her page settle into her mind. She had been through so much with God lately, witnessing Him bind up her broken heart and her marriage began to heal because of it. The more Tamara became a woman of the Word, the less she agreed with the things going on around her, yet she would still go along to keep the peace, compromising her beliefs. Tamara's heart hurt as she realized her actions showed she cared more about pleasing people than pleasing God. Tamara feared being apart from people more than being apart from God. She saw how often her real motive with others was to gain their acceptance or approval, not to honor God with her actions.

As truth dawned in her heart, Tamara repented for valuing her reputation among her peers over her relationship with God. She asked God to forgive her and to give her the courage to follow through with the commands the Holy Spirit was teaching her. Tamara wanted to learn to be faithful to God. She knew lots of things in her life needed to change, starting with removing the things that caused the most separation from God. By cutting out social media, Tamara discovered she didn't find herself casting judgment on others as often, because she wasn't focused on someone else's life in place of her own. She dedicated the time she would have spent on social media to spending extra time in the Word and tuning in to her husband and children—the time was so rich and always fruitful! Tamara hadn't realized how much time she was spending reading about other people's lives, and all the while hers was literally passing her by!

As this settled in, she wondered what other safe boundaries she may need to set concerning the protection of her heart, soul, and mind. It was going to take self-control and faith, but she wanted to get her priorities straight! Tamara added up her waking hours outside of work. She then went down the list of the things she gave time to each week. When she added up the amount of time spent engaged with her family versus the top two things on her list, her heart broke. The truth was, God and her family got the least amount of her time most days. She had some serious choices to make! Praying for guidance, she asked God to continue to reveal things she had valued over spending time with Him.

The more time Tamara spent with God, the less she found herself desiring things from her past. God was rewriting her heart to desire Him on greater levels. It was as if the Holy Spirit was stoking the flame of desire inside her as she purposed to put away the things He brought to her attention.

Trust

You are not likely to fully trust someone you don't know, and you can't walk in unbroken fellowship with someone you don't trust. Now that you are moving into a relationship with Jesus that is built on trust, you are growing into the type of worshipper the Father is seeking—a woman who trusts God's love for her, even when she feels like she doesn't measure up or when she can't feel His closeness.

When I first started learning what worshipping God in Spirit and truth meant, I understood it would take time for me to genuinely grow into the kind of worshipper God wanted me to be. I couldn't fake it, and it had nothing to do with whether or not I raised my hands in the worship service on Sunday and everything to do with my heart and the choices I made, moment by moment, every day. Did the choices I made glorify God? Forget about the people watching me; this was first about my Father and me. Were my choices, thoughts, words, and actions proving my love for Jesus or myself? Who was my idol—Jesus or things that pleased my flesh and got me more followers on Facebook? This was a new concept for me, and it seemed I had a lot of work ahead!

Even though it has been a process, I have not missed the things I gave up. God honored my obedience, and I found joy in simple things again. I fell passionately in love with my Father, and I found a new desire to learn to be the wife and mother He created me to be. I began to spend more time in the Word caring for my spiritual health than I did in the gym working on my physical appearance. I needed balance in my life, and God helped me find it when I made Him my top priority. Instead of finding my value in my career or my physical appearance, He became my value and my worship. Do you see how this works?

TURN AWAY FROM THE THINGS THAT LEAD YOU AWAY!

Do you ever just want to raise your hand and ask God if you can have a "redo?" You know, a fresh start? Well, that is only one of the best things about our Heavenly Father! Like the story with Tamara, when He sees our hearts broken and contrite over sin and we repent, He wipes the slate clean, remembering it no more. I pray that by now you have learned the value of God's presence in your life—not like you used to, but on a deeper, real-life level.

I pray you have come to truly understand that God IS alive, and He desires a real-life relationship with you. This process has been very strategic in hopefully leading you into an undeniable reality with God, so that now you can look back at your life and determine the areas where you are half-hearted for God instead of whole-hearted—first commandment style—for Him. You would not have been able to see these areas in the beginning because, in your heart, you didn't know why it was important to turn away from certain things. Now, however, you have been experiencing God on deeper levels than before, enabling you to value what He values because you experienced His goodness in the private, hurt places of your heart.

Addressing idols is not about Mosaic law—the law that required sacrifice for sins, but the law of love. This is the law that Jesus came and fulfilled. When we ask God to show us things we do in our daily lives that do not show our love for

Him, we are saying, "More of you, God, less of me!" Don't you want that? I know I do—so much so, that I am willing to allow the Holy Spirit to come in and reveal my habits that do not glorify God. However, without knowing the Scriptures, including the Old Testament, I wouldn't understand why these things were important. God is good, and we know the things He asks of us are not pointless. They are for His glory and for our protection from being drawn away from Him.

> **GOING THROUGH THE MOTIONS DOESN'T PLEASE YOU, A FLAWLESS PERFORMANCE IS NOTHING TO YOU. I LEARNED GOD-WORSHIP WHEN MY PRIDE WAS SHATTERED. HEART-SHATTERED LIVES READY FOR LOVE DON'T FOR A MOMENT ESCAPE GOD'S NOTICE.**
> **—PSALM 51:16-17 MSG**

Jesus Is My "Unwind"

The things that rob you of your affections for God aren't just the surface expressions, like social media, gym, alcohol, or tuning out with movies and television. Those things are the physical manifestations of your spiritual strongholds. The idols you have in your life are both anchored to, and the result of, strongholds in your mind. A stronghold is anything that sets itself up against the knowledge of God (see 2 Corinthians 10:5).

When we tune out from God, we hurt ourselves. When you and I truly tune in to the Father's love, we never want or need a break from Him. He becomes our "unwind." How can tuning into the world ever provide mental rest and feed your spirit? It can't.

The passions in your heart are driven by an innate knowledge as your soul searches for the One for whom it was made—the Father. However, when you continue to fill that space with knowledge and experiences from the world that opposes the will of God, over time, it creates strongholds in your thought patterns about what is acceptable and what isn't, who you are and who you are not, what you are and

DO YOUR CHOICES THOUGHTS, WORDS, AND ACTIONS SHOW YOUR LOVE FOR JESUS OR YOURSELF?

are not capable of. This is the root of the desires for things that cause you to look away from Him, seeking fulfillment and satisfaction elsewhere, when what you are really seeking can only come from the One who created you.

Though your idols are a problem, they are not the primary problem. The fundamental problem is the stronghold that allowed them. This is why what you choose to let into your mind is so important! I could tell you to put your idols away and, if you agreed, you might be successful for a time . . . However, without the root of the idol removed, it will find its way back to the surface, or another will replace it. These roots or strongholds are torn down as you begin feeding your spirit the food it was designed for: The Word of God. This is how we become the kind of worshipper the Father is seeking.

> ### AS THE FATHER HAS LOVED ME, SO HAVE I LOVED YOU.
> ### NOW REMAIN IN MY LOVE.
> ### —JOHN 15:9 NIV

The Samaritan Woman

JOHN 4:4-42 NIV

[1]Now Jesus learned that the pharisees had heard that he was gaining and baptizing more disciples than John— [2]although in fact it was not Jesus who baptized, but his disciples. [3]So he left Judea and went back once more to galilee.

[4] Now he had to go through Samaria. [5]So he came to a town in Samaria called Sychar, near the plot of ground Jacob had given to his son Joseph. [6]Jacob's well was there, and Jesus, tired as he was from the journey, sat down by the well. It was about noon.

[7]When a samaritan woman came to draw water, Jesus said to her, "will you give me a drink?" [8](His disciples had gone into the town to buy food.)

[9]The samaritan woman said to him, "you are a Jew and I am a samaritan woman. How can you ask me for a drink?" (For Jews do not associate with samaritans.)

[10]Jesus answered her, "if you knew the gift of God and who it is that asks you for a drink, you would have asked Him and He would have given you living water."

¹¹"Sir," the woman said, "you have nothing to draw with and the well is deep. Where can you get this living water? ¹²Are you greater than our father Jacob, who gave us the well and drank from it himself, as did also his sons and his livestock?"

¹³ Jesus answered, "everyone who drinks this water will be thirsty again, ¹⁴but whoever drinks the water I give them will never thirst. Indeed, the water I give them will become in them a spring of water welling up to eternal life."

¹⁵The woman said to him, "sir, give me this water so that I won't get thirsty and have to keep coming here to draw water."

¹⁶He told her, "go, call your husband and come back."

¹⁷"I have no husband," she replied.

Jesus said to her, "you are right when you say you have no husband. ¹⁸The fact is, you have had five husbands, and the man you now have is not your husband. What you have just said is quite true."

¹⁹"Sir," the woman said, "I can see that you are a prophet. ²⁰Our ancestors worshiped on this mountain, but you Jews claim that the place where we must worship is in Jerusalem."

²¹"Woman," Jesus replied, "believe me, a time is coming when you will worship the Father neither on this mountain nor in Jerusalem. ²²You samaritans worship what you do not know; we worship what we do know, for salvation is from the Jews. ²³Yet a time is coming and has now come when the true worshipers will worship the Father in the spirit and in truth, for they are the kind of worshipers the Father seeks. ²⁴God is spirit, and his worshipers must worship in the spirit and in truth."

²⁵The woman said, "I know that messiah" (called Christ) "is coming. When He comes, He will explain everything to us."

²⁶Then Jesus declared, "I, the one speaking to you—I am he."

²⁷Just then his disciples returned and were surprised to find him talking with a woman. But no one asked, "what do you want?" Or "why are you talking with her?"

²⁸Then, leaving her water jar, the woman went back to the town and said to the people, ²⁹"come, see a man who told me everything I ever did. Could this be the Messiah?" ³⁰They came out of the town and made their way toward Him.

³¹Meanwhile His disciples urged him, "Rabbi, eat something."

³²But he said to them, "I have food to eat that you know nothing about."

³³Then his disciples said to each other, "could someone have brought him food?"

³⁴"My food," said Jesus, "is to do the will of Him who sent me and to finish His work. ³⁵Don't you have a saying, 'it's still four months until harvest'? I tell you, open your eyes and look at the fields! They are ripe for harvest. ³⁶Even now the one who reaps draws a wage and harvests a crop for eternal life, so that the sower and the reaper may be glad together. ³⁷Thus the saying 'one sows and another reaps' is true. ³⁸I sent you to reap what you have not worked for. Others have done the hard work, and you have reaped the benefits of their labor."

³⁹Many of the samaritans from that town believed in Him because of the woman's testimony, "He told me everything I ever did." ⁴⁰So when the samaritans came to Him, they urged Him to stay with them, and He stayed two days. ⁴¹And because of His words many more became believers.

⁴²They said to the woman, "we no longer believe just because of what you said; now we have heard for ourselves, and we know that this man really is the savior of the world."

A WOMAN IN NEED OF LIVING WATER

You may not know what it means to feel like an outcast or to be unaccepted, but many do. Throughout Scripture, you often find Jesus with the afflicted and outcasts of society. The Samaritan woman was one of these.

The fact that she was at the well drawing water around noon shows she was likely an outcast (see John 4:6). I imagine because of this woman's history with men and the way she was viewed around town, that she wasn't a part of the cliques of women who hung out at the waterhole before the sun would cause sweat to bead on their foreheads. I'd say this woman came at a later hour to avoid the judgmental looks and fake smiles—which can often cut just as deep as a rude comment. However, when Jesus came along, there was no division between the Samaritan woman and Himself. He asked her to serve Him (see John 4:7). It seems clear the woman felt too worthless even to serve a Jewish man a drink of water, forget the fact that the one in front of her was the Messiah (see John 4:9)!

What Jesus was offering was eternal value and worth that only comes through belief; it cannot be earned or lost by an action (see John 4:10-15). Jesus told her everything she had ever done, which led to her conviction and belief in who He was. This was when He began to restore her worth and value. He tore away even the label that demeaned her race when He explained that worship was a posture of the heart of a believer, not something that could only be found on a mountain top or in a hierarchy of race or religion. She too, could be the type of worshipper the Father was seeking!

The woman took off into town to tell the townspeople about the man who had convicted her. Jesus had restored her value and worth. We know this because first, she felt confident enough to go and tell the townspeople about the Messiah! And secondly, verses 30 and 39 say the townspeople listened to her and made their way toward Jesus, and then many were saved because of her testimony! The whole town listened to her testimony, and revival broke out in Samaria! In one conversation, Jesus stripped this woman of anything that devalued her and gave back what the enemy had stolen—her identity. As if that wasn't enough—revival broke out, and many people were saved!

Today, she may look like the Christian woman who has been divorced many times, the woman with piercings and blue hair, or someone finding her way to Jesus from another belief system. She represents the woman you may find yourself easily judging and looking down on.

I liken the water from the well in Samaria to the surface expressions of the things that rob us of our affections for God. This kind of water only quenches our physical thirst—the passions and desires of our flesh. It's deceiving because of how it hides the deeper thirst within by meeting the material desires of the flesh. It doesn't take much effort to get, and it is neither pure nor holy. However, the water Jesus offers quenches a deep and eternal thirst because it flows straight from the Father. The acceptance Jesus offers us isn't conditional or temporary. It doesn't pass through the body to be discarded as waste. His nourishment seeps into the bones, wasting nothing, healing, and bringing life.

What Gives You a False Sense of Value?

Sometimes when we read Scripture, we think of "worshipping idols" or "idolatry" as having an actual golden calf in a secret room in our house or something dedicated to witchcraft. Idols are rarely that obvious! Most often they are rooted in strongholds—a wrong thought process that drives you to seek affirmation for your self-worth outside of Jesus Christ. An idol is anything you put ahead of your relationship with God.

What or whom do you desire more than God (examples: spouse, children, parents, self, beauty, friends, job, material things, pleasing others, money, acceptance, etc.,)?

What do you fear more than God (examples: rejection, failure, being poor, not being pleasing, etc.,)?

What or whom do you trust more than God (examples: husband, money, health insurance, the government, your boss, job, paycheck, etc.)?

What occupies most of your thoughts throughout the day and night?

What occupies most of your time throughout the day?

Grace will save a man . . .
But it will not save him and his idol.
—A.W. Tozer

Grace is the mercy of God given to people who did nothing to deserve it. It is only out of His kindness that He gives us the power to live out what His Word demands of us. God's grace provides us with the power to resist sin, not an excuse to walk in it.

THOSE WHO CLING TO WORTHLESS IDOLS TURN AWAY FROM GOD'S LOVE FOR THEM.
—JONAH 2:8 NIV

I understand certain situations are more difficult than others, like taking care of aging parents, special needs children, or even a demanding job. However, there is a healthy balance for everything. No matter what the circumstance, whether you need self-control with television, social media, or healthy boundaries for how to grow spiritually in the midst of whatever battle you are facing, ask God for His help. He understands your circumstance, and He wastes nothing. He must be your top priority for healthy living. He will help you find a balance no matter your circumstance, and He will not ask more of you than you can give!

How does Scripture define "noble character?" (Acts 17:11 NIV84)

I NEED TO NEED YOU, FATHER...

JAMES 4:4-10 NKJV

[4]Adulterers and adulteresses! Do you not know that friendship with the world is enmity with God? Whoever therefore wants to be a friend of the world makes himself an enemy of God. [5] Or do you think that the Scripture says in vain, "The Spirit who dwells in us yearns jealously"?

[6] But He gives more grace. Therefore He says:

"God resists the proud,

But gives grace to the humble."

[7] Therefore submit to God. Resist the devil and he will flee from you. [8] Draw near to God and He will draw near to you. Cleanse your hands, you sinners; and purify your hearts, you double-minded. [9] Lament and mourn and weep! Let your laughter be turned to mourning and your joy to gloom. [10] Humble yourselves in the sight of the Lord, and He will lift you up.

ROMANS 7:15-20 NLT

[15] I don't really understand myself, for I want to do what is right, but I don't do it. Instead, I do what I hate. [16] But if I know that what I am doing is wrong, this shows that I agree that the law is good. [17] So I am not the one doing wrong; it is sin living in me that does it.

[18] And I know that nothing good lives in me, that is, in my sinful nature. I want to do what is right, but I can't. [19] I want to do what is good, but I don't. I don't want to do what is wrong, but I do it anyway. [20] But if I do what I don't want to do, I am not really the one doing wrong; it is sin living in me that does it.

RECITE THE PRAYER BELOW AS YOU AGREE IN YOUR HEART.

Prayer:

> *Father, help me to put down the things that keep me from You. Awaken new depths in me so I may walk deeper in Your righteousness. Father, You are my loving Heavenly Father, and You are always in pursuit of me. I freely give You my empire here on earth, these things that I hold on to and turn to that aren't You—the empire of my heart, soul, and mind. My thoughts, my emotions, my self-control—I give it to You. I give my control to You; my life is Yours to guide and lead and protect. Father, I am Yours.*

Forgive me for the things I have put ahead of You, like:

I give You the things I think I deserve, like:

Forgive me for the things I worry about and the things I fear, like:

Forgive me for giving all of my energy to:

Forgive me for the times I have not trusted You, but trusted:

Father,

May I value my place in the Kingdom more than I value my place in this world. May Your Kingdom come in my life here on earth as it is in heaven. May Your will be done in my life today and every day. May I spread Your Kingdom and not myself. More of You, less of me.

Review

1. When re-evaluating what is important in your life, ask good questions:

2. Does this habit or choice bring me closer to God or lead me away from God?

3. Does this habit or choice benefit my family in a godly way or not?

4. Does this habit or choice make my husband feel valued and pursued by me, or pushed off to the side and rejected?

5. Turn away from the things that led you away.

Main Take-Away

What was your main take-away from this lesson?

Before Your Next Meeting

1. Try to have a Quiet Time at least four times this week using the verses listed for Lesson 6.

2. Come prepared having finished Lesson 6.

3. Memorize **John 15:9-10** this week.

Notes

CULTIVATING

Holy Beauty

Women's Authentic Discipleship
It's That Simple!

Everything You Need to Get Connected!

*Register with CHB to Get Updates on
New Book Releases, Events, and Other News!*

Help us connect women looking to join a Cultivating Holy Beauty group in your area!
Scan code to register!

www.CultivatingHolyBeauty.com/Register

Training Videos for Leaders

Scan code to learn more about starting a CHB group and for answers to
commonly asked questions!

https://youtube.com/channel/UCbq_TztU9UDVAazw-OLVy7g

A Woman After God's Own Heart

KEY POINT

This lesson builds on forgiveness, showing you how to turn to God first before you entertain lies that may become strongholds. The result is you are then able to agree with God's thoughts about yourself, instead of your old thought patterns.

WHY THIS MATTERS

When we allow God to identify the strongholds and idols we have in our lives that hold us captive in our seemingly silent sin, we live in greater freedom.

HOW TO APPLY

Scripture says, those who love God, keep His commands. We prove our love for God when we purpose to follow His ways above our own.

LESSON 6

A Woman After God's Own Heart

MEMORY VERSES

John 15:9-10 (Write your memory verse in the space below.)

QUIET TIME VERSES

John 15:1-12; Psalm 19:12-14; Romans 8:1-17; 2 Corinthians 10:3-5; Psalm 38:9-11; Ephesians 4:20-32; John 4:1-38

Complete Lesson 6 and try to have four to seven Quiet Times before your next meeting. To ensure you are using the verse in the correct context, be sure to read several verses before and after the suggested Quiet Time passage(s).

KEY POINT

This lesson builds on forgiveness, showing you how to turn to God first before you entertain lies that may become strongholds. The result is you are then able to agree with God's thoughts about yourself, instead of your old thought patterns.

WHY THIS MATTERS

When we allow God to identify the strongholds and idols we have in our lives that hold us captive in our seemingly silent sin, we live in greater freedom.

HOW TO APPLY

Scripture says, those who love God, keep His commands. We prove our love for God when we purpose to follow His ways above our own.

Leader's Notes

- This lesson may take more than one or two weeks. If a group member has to miss causing the group to sit longer than two weeks in a lesson, find a time to meet with her one-on-one or over the phone so the group can keep moving forward.

- PRAY for your group to begin to chase after the deeper things of God's heart, without concern for world's condemnation. Be faithful to encourage them; they will need your prayer covering!

- Highlight one or two questions from the lesson to be discussed in group time, allowing each person to share an answer. For quick reference, write the page numbers of the questions you chose to discuss below.

Navigating Your Group Time

- Spend 15-20 minutes in worship.

- As the time of worship comes to a close, the leader should begin the WAR method of prayer.

- Write a quick summary of Lesson 6 in the space below. Share this with the group to begin the lesson after the time of prayer is finished

- Have group members share their "Main Take-Away" from the end of the lesson.

- Have each person share a Quiet Time.

- If time allows, have each person share an answer from the questions the leader highlighted (1-2 questions).

- Read sections: "Review" and "Before Your Next Lesson".

- Break into pairs and recite your verses.

- Remind everyone to sign off on each other's course record in the back of the book.

LESSON 6

A Woman After God's Own Heart

MEMORY VERSES

John 15:9-10 (Write your memory verse in the space below.)

QUIET TIME VERSES

John 15:1-12; Psalm 19:12-14; Romans 8:1-17; 2 Corinthians 10:3-5; Psalm 38:9-11; Ephesians 4:20-32; John 4:1-38

Complete Lesson 6 and try to have four to seven Quiet Times before your next meeting. To ensure you are using the verse in the correct context, be sure to read several verses before and after the suggested Quiet Time passage(s).

KEY POINT

This lesson builds on forgiveness, showing you how to turn to God first before you entertain lies that may become strongholds. The result is you are then able to agree with God's thoughts about yourself, instead of your old thought patterns.

WHY THIS MATTERS

When we allow God to identify the strongholds and idols we have in our lives that hold us captive in our seemingly silent sin, we live in greater freedom.

HOW TO APPLY

Scripture says, those who love God, keep His commands. We prove our love for God when we purpose to follow His ways above our own.

Participant's Notes

- Use a concordance, dictionary, and thesaurus to go deeper in your Quiet Time.

- Complete this lesson before your next meeting. Be sure to answer the questions marked with a discussion bubble ⬭ and be ready to share your answers with the group. It's important to remember there are no wrong answers to the questions throughout the lessons because they are your thoughts, so be free in how you answer!

- PRAY for your group to begin to chase after the deeper things of God's heart, without concern for the world's condemnation. Be faithful to encourage them; they will need your prayer covering!

- Use the space provided in the margins to take notes, write down additional Scripture references you find, or to draw pictures that come to mind as you journey through "A Woman After God's Own Heart."

A Woman After God's Own Heart

As I moved through the editing process of this material, I looked for spiritually mature women and men of all ages to read through the lessons. I wanted to make sure the spiritual truths were clear and, of course, doctrinally sound. A friend of mine, who travels with her husband as he counsels pastors, wrote to me with this suggestion:

Jessie,

Some women who have the same type of hurts and sins may not see them as such because they don't come from backgrounds like the women in the stories of "Letting the Healer Heal." The ones who come from healthy families and have no real problems in their marriages . . .

Two examples: A lady in a church in Salt Lake City years ago had three children. She had a terrible time trying to parent. There was no real issue in her marriage or even the way she was raised . . . but she kept second-guessing herself. Finally, she related that her toddler had drawn on her walls and she was extremely distraught— much more so than most would have been. Her hurt was from trying to be perfect and falling short. I cannot remember if her family was extremely legalistic, she honestly wanted to do what was right, but to the extreme. She found herself trying to be perfect in all that she did. This seems so minor compared to what you have shared in Book 2, but I have dealt with many women who have similar issues. She could not understand that what she was doing was sinful . . . not in the legalistic way she guarded against, but in trying to live up to a standard that was not what God intended, but had been dictated by someone to her somewhere along the way. I could see how my friend may not relate to the stories you shared in Book 2 because of the way she saw herself. In fact, she would be heartbroken for the ladies, but would not see that what she was dealing with was a similar sin.

Then, there is the lady who cannot get past condemning. This lady had lived what she considered to be a "really great Christian life." She was involved in Bible study and even taught at times. She worked in the nursery and taught children's Sunday School. Her problem was that anyone who was less than perfect or had committed sin as you related, would be written off as "untouchable." This is a very real sin that needs to be dealt with in churches today. How can the Lord use us when we are so busy condemning others for their sin? Interestingly, great influential

Christian ladies could not stop being immoral until they came to know and trust Jesus deeply. This condemning lady had no problem with the author of the Bible study we were doing at the time because she loved the author, but she could not, or would not, forgive others who were in her circle of acquaintances. Her background was one that was extremely rigid . . . "Follow the rules and Jesus will be more pleased with you." She struggled with a loving relationship with Jesus. The issue was that she did not see herself as needing more. Writing Love Letters to Jesus would be entirely out of her comfort zone and something that she would struggle with, yet she really needs to understand that her sin of condemning others keeps her from truly knowing Jesus.

Both ladies would consider themselves to be good, Christian ladies. Neither would see themselves as committing any of the sins you discussed. Yet, they both had deep hurts that neither could understand. Neither functioned well in the church. The second lady had never really been "happy" in church because she could not let go of unforgiveness.

Anyway, something to chew on and bring before Jesus.

Sincerely,

Lois

My wise friend was right (see Titus 2: 3-5; 1 Timothy 5:24)! It is crucial to understand that God cares about your seemingly "minor" issues as much as He does the more obvious ones. Jesus came to bind up the brokenhearted and set captives free (see Isaiah 61). There is no stipulation that says, "This only applies to the ones who are really hurting." This gift is for ALL of God's children. When you put your identity in Jesus, you lose your insecurities, no longer living in offense of what others lack—but coming up underneath them and pointing them to Jesus . . . helping them in their weaknesses instead of judging them for it.

The Word of God is not here as a tool for us to analyze each other. Instead, it is here for us to be examined by it. When we allow God this freedom in our hearts, we begin to live life by the Spirit. The majority of Christians live in spiritual deficit. Whether you grew up churched or unchurched is not the question. If you have been living life by the rules of the flesh and not genuinely governed by the Spirit of the Living Word, you are in spiritual deficit. Romans 8:1 says, "There is now no condemnation for those who are in Christ Jesus because through Jesus Christ, the law of the Spirit of life set me free from the law of sin and death." Here it is, written in plain sight. The things we choose that are of the flesh lead us away from God, but the things we choose that are of the Spirit bring us closer to God. Choosing to allow this process to happen in your life is the process of sanctification.

Strong's Concordance lists sanctification as purification of the heart and life. This is what living by the Spirit means. It is a process; it doesn't happen all at once. It takes time and hard work. However, it is in that precious wrestle that you see God's faithfulness to you, and you begin trusting in His love.

To grow in your belief of who God is and His love for you—which is all that matters—you must continue to allow the Word to cultivate your heart. There is no other way to accomplish this, and this process never stops. This requires digging deep into the Word and allowing it to dig deep into you. Removing bitter root systems and pruning branches of good trees is the process of sanctification. It means growing closer to God, and while it may be what we all want, it's hard to put away the desires of our human nature for the promises of God which can sometimes seem so far away.

SANCTIFICATION PRODUCES PURIFICATION WHICH INCREASES HOLY BEAUTY.

Remember, the enemy is nothing but a lie that comes to separate you from the knowledge of God's love for you. If he can get you believing God has more important priorities than you and your struggles, or the mundane things you choose every day over God just aren't that big of a deal, then you eventually become isolated and easy prey for deception.

The enemy is continuously working to discredit God in your life. He does this subtly, by planting a tiny seed of jealousy, inadequacy, judgment, intellectualism, legalism, condemnation, etc., in your mind. Over time it grows quietly under the surface, reaching the depths of your heart. If the enemy was unable to take you down in the more blatantly obvious ways, as described in some of the stories shared through the pages of *Cultivating Holy Beauty*, he will take his time with a stealthier approach, like leaving and coming back later when your guard is down (see Luke 4:13). God doesn't require extravagant things from you for you to be called "His." He just wants your love (see Matthew 22:36-38).

Ask God to help you with the following questions:

Think about yourself where God is concerned. Is there anything you feel you have to accomplish to receive His approval or affection?

What is the only thing God wants from you? (Hint: see Matthew 22:36-38)

Is it possible that you put a higher standard on yourself than God does?

What does God desire from others?

Do you put a higher standard on others than God does? Do you require more of others than God Himself desires from them?

If so, explain what this looks like:

How might your relationship with others change if you purposed to give to others what God desires from you (see Matthew 22:39)?

Embracing God's Plan

Since the beginning of mankind, God has allowed us to make our own choices. This means we get to choose what we value! Due to past circumstances, you may have felt like you didn't have a choice in what you learned to value, but that was in the past, and it is not the case today! After cleaning out your heart of what may have been decades of hurt and pain, it is important to now learn who you are in Jesus and bond with the person God created you to be.

The grid through which you used to see things has changed because the infection has been cleaned out of your heart; the sickly fevered haze from your spiritual heart infection has burned off, if you will. Now you'll learn to see yourself, God, and life in general, more the way God intended. Isn't it exciting to realize that when we truly repent from a pure heart, our slate is wiped clean?!

SISTER, YOU HAVE GOD'S PERMISSION TO LET GO OF THE OLD AND WALK IN THE NEW!

When I went through a journey of healing from my past, I realized I wasn't sure what to do with myself after that. It was as if there was a little person inside that I didn't really know very well. The true me—the healed me—was the part of me that loved Jesus with everything she had and wanted to serve Him with her whole life! For decades, it seemed I had been hiding and fighting for an identity that I never really wanted in the first place. It was all I had known—until Jesus bound up my wounds and set my captive heart free! So what was I going to value now? And how was I going to train myself in this "value system"? Could it really be as simple as a choice to learn and purpose God's way in place of my own? I was fixing to find out!

Jesus said, "If you abide in My Word, you are truly My disciples, and you will know the Truth, and the Truth will set you free." (John 8:31-32 ESV) This is how we walk in freedom . . . "the new," by abiding in His Word and choosing truth over lies! Through His Word we will know truth and experience lasting freedom—it's a promise!

CULTIVATE THESE THINGS. IMMERSE YOURSELF IN THEM.
THE PEOPLE WILL ALL SEE YOU MATURE RIGHT BEFORE THEIR
EYES! KEEP A FIRM GRASP ON BOTH YOUR CHARACTER
AND YOUR TEACHING. DON'T BE DIVERTED. JUST KEEP
AT IT. BOTH YOU AND THOSE WHO HEAR
YOU WILL EXPERIENCE SALVATION.
—1 TIMOTHY 4:15-16 MSG

LEARNING TO BE SENSITIVE TO THE SPIRIT OF GOD AND WHY IT MATTERS

READ EPHESIANS 4 AND 5.

In his book, "Sensitive to the Spirit," RT Kendal wrote, "When you grieve the Holy Spirit through things listed in Scripture, it's like the 'sense of God' seems to lift." Though He doesn't really leave—because Jesus promised He would be with us forever—sometimes it can certainly feel that way (see John 14:16)! So how do you keep that from happening? Well, we must agree with God that it's impossible to get it right and keep it right as long as we are not in a glorified body with the resurrected Christ in Glory. However, by knowing the Word of God, you learn what grieves the Spirit.

The "sense" of feeling distant from God is a precautionary measure God has put in place for those who care to notice. When I feel this distance come upon me, I start backtracking and seeking the Lord to see if I have grieved Him. Am I so arrogant to believe there is no sin in me and that I have done nothing wrong (see 1 John 1:8)?

At times, however, I don't recognize my sin, but God, being the loving Father that He is, reaches for me by letting me feel the distance between us. I pray I never forget what it felt like to be apart from God when I was lost; it drives me harder to His feet when I'm reminded. It is a very effective method for those who love Him!

Again, if Jesus said it was wrong, then don't do it! End of story! Sin has to matter to you, enough that you stop doing it because you can't stand the feeling of His Spirit lifting. He doesn't turn his back on you and me; we turn our back on Him (see 1 Timothy 4:1; Hebrews 6:4-6). Allow Him to be your only comparison for what you use to justify your actions and your worth. No job can do that, no famous singer or actor, no pastor, no husband, no other human, no amount of money . . . nothing and no one—only Jesus. The heart of God is your fortress and refuge. It's the only place you are truly safe and secure.

This "sense" is mentioned in Scripture over and over again; here is one of the more famous examples:

BEHOLD, THE LORD'S HAND IS NOT SHORTENED, THAT IT
CANNOT SAVE, OR HIS EAR DULL, THAT IT CANNOT HEAR;
BUT YOUR INIQUITIES HAVE MADE A SEPARATION BETWEEN
YOU AND YOUR GOD, AND YOUR SINS HAVE HIDDEN HIS
FACE FROM YOU SO THAT HE DOES NOT HEAR.
—ISAIAH 59:1-2 ESV

True worship of God is purposing to do what He says is right, and not doing what He says is wrong because no matter how hard it seems and not because He desires sacrifice—He doesn't (see 1 Samuel 15:22). Worship is a posture of the heart—a response of gratitude to our Savior. This is the measure of true worship because it reflects the condition of your heart. When you purpose to turn from immoral passions of the flesh, due to the thought of being apart from Him who is Holy, you are worshipping the Father in Spirit and Truth. The appropriate heart attitude toward both the Word and the Holy Spirit produces this kind of worship.

Paul mentions "circumcision" in Philippians 3:3. This refers to the condition of your heart toward spiritual impurity—according to Strong's definition (see Romans 2:29 also). There are no physical works that can achieve this. However, the actions of a believer with a circumcised heart are vastly different because it's an overflow of the fruit of their relationship with God, not a means to get closer to God.

Summarize the paragraph above in your own words.

ASSIGNMENT

I share my Love Letters from God with you so that you can build a box for how the Lord wants to speak to you. Be willing to hear His thoughts for you. God made you precisely the way you are; it took thought and creativity. Are we to dictate what God will and will not do, what He will and will not say? He is the same today as He was yesterday. He is only limited in your life by your unbelief.

Daughter,

Keep seeking Me, little daughter. Keep seeking this relationship with Me. Keep being My daughter, My galaxy dancer—twirling with all of your shimmering colors. You are human, and you will fall, but when you fall, know you are still Mine. When you fall short of all you intend to be, you are still Mine. These times reveal My faithfulness to you. These times reveal My nature to you. You are Mine, even when you feel like you don't belong. When you were wandering and looking for Me, the world overcame you. You could not see or hear Me. Your spirit had dirty, tear-streaked cheeks; your dress was tattered—you felt so lost. The lies were getting too loud, and it was hard for you to tell what was truth and what was lies. Many times you turned toward the lies, but we have dealt with those, and you are forgiven. You were wandering blindly in the wilderness, and finally, you heard Me, and you turned toward Me. You chose not to lay in the bed the world had made for you. You lept from it and ran to Me. Little daughter, you sought Me and fought for your life when you chose Me. You sought Me when you laid down your own strong will and surrendered to Me. Keep seeking Me, little daughter. When you fail, expect to see My face, not My back. Expect not just My hands reaching for you, but My arms to embrace you. Delight in Me as I delight in you. I want to feel your love, little one who uses galaxies for stepping stones. I have made you to feel Me. It's time for you to comprehend My love for you.

Love,

Your Abba

Learning to be a woman after God's own heart means continuing to work on forgiving yourself and others while allowing God to speak His truth to you. Continue making yourself available to the Lord—quieting your soul before Him. Purpose to trust His loving truth as much as you believed the lies of the past.

Why do you need to be willing to listen to the Holy Spirit with your heart?

Why is it important to trust what you hear?

What are you afraid of when it comes to hearing from the Lord? Write out a prayer to the Lord bringing your fears into the light. Remember, you will be able to anchor anything you hear from the Holy Spirit with Scripture.

Write down any lies you may be hearing. Then practice flipping them for truth and anchoring the truth with Scripture.

Love Letter from God

 ## Review

1. True worship of God is purposing to do what He says is right, and not doing what He says is wrong—no matter how hard it seems.

2. Learning to be a woman after God's own heart means continuing to work on forgiving yourself and others while allowing God to speak His truth to you.

3. Allow Jesus to be your only comparison.

4. The "circumcision" mentioned in Philippians 3:3 refers to the condition of your heart toward spiritual impurity.

 ## Main Take-Away

What was your main take-away from this lesson?

 ## Before Your Next Meeting

1. Try to have a Quiet Time at least four times this week using the verses listed for Lesson 7.

2. Memorize **James 1:22** this week.

Notes

Notes

Anchored

KEY POINT

Knowing Scripture and knowing how to apply Scripture are not the same thing. What makes you a woman of the Word is that you are applying the Word to your life and doing what it says.

WHY THIS MATTERS

Learning how to apply Scripture to your daily battles helps you grow in your faith.

HOW TO APPLY

Personalize your battle strategy! Just "knowing" the Word glorifies yourself, however, doing the Word glorifies the Lord.

Leader's Guide

LESSON 7

Anchored

MEMORY VERSES

James 1:22 (Write your memory verse in the space below.)

QUIET TIME VERSES

James 1:18-25; Hosea 4:6-7; 1 Corinthians 12:1-3; Psalm 119:89-96; 1 Peter 2:1-3; Luke 24:1-53; Hebrews 4:12-13

Complete Lesson 7 and try to have four to seven Quiet Times before your next meeting. To ensure you are using the verse in the correct context, be sure to read several verses before and after the suggested Quiet Time passage(s).

KEY POINT

Knowing Scripture and knowing how to apply Scripture are not the same thing. What makes you a woman of the Word is that you are applying the Word to your life and doing what it says.

WHY THIS MATTERS

Learning how to apply Scripture to your daily battles helps you grow in your faith.

HOW TO APPLY

Personalize your battle strategy! Just "knowing" the Word glorifies yourself, however, doing the Word glorifies the Lord.

Leader's Notes

- This lesson may take more than one or two weeks. If a group member has to miss causing the group to sit longer than two weeks in a lesson, find a time to meet with her one-on-one or over the phone so the group can keep moving forward.

- PRAY for your group to take being anchored in the Word to a whole new level!

- Highlight one or two questions from the lesson to be discussed in group time, allowing each person to share an answer. For quick reference, write the page numbers of the questions you chose to discuss below.

Navigating Your Group Time

- Spend 15-20 minutes in worship.

- As the time of worship comes to a close, the leader should begin the WAR method of prayer.

- Write a quick summary of Lesson 7 in the space below. Share this with the group to begin the lesson after the time of prayer is finished

- Have group members share their "Main Take-Away" from the end of the lesson.

- Have each person share a Quiet Time.

- If time allows, have each person share an answer from the questions the leader highlighted (1-2 questions).

- Read sections: "Review" and "Before Your Next Lesson".

- Break into pairs and recite your verses.

- Remind everyone to sign off on each other's course record in the back of the book.

LESSON 7

Anchored

MEMORY VERSES

James 1:22 (Write your memory verse in the space below.)

QUIET TIME VERSES

James 1:18-25; Hosea 4:6-7; 1 Corinthians 12:1-3; Psalm 119:89-96; 1 Peter 2:1-3; Luke 24:1-53; Hebrews 4:12-13

Complete Lesson 7 and try to have four to seven Quiet Times before your next meeting. To ensure you are using the verse in the correct context, be sure to read several verses before and after the suggested Quiet Time passage(s).

KEY POINT

Knowing Scripture and knowing how to apply Scripture are not the same thing. What makes you a woman of the Word is that you are applying the Word to your life and doing what it says.

WHY THIS MATTERS

Learning how to apply Scripture to your daily battles helps you grow in your faith.

HOW TO APPLY

Personalize your battle strategy! Just "knowing" the Word glorifies yourself, however, doing the Word glorifies the Lord.

Participant's Notes

- Complete this lesson before your next meeting. Be sure to answer the questions marked with a discussion bubble 🗨 and be ready to share your answers with the group. It's important to remember there are no wrong answers to the questions throughout the lessons because they are your thoughts, so be free in how you answer!

- PRAY for yourself and your fellow group members to take being anchored in the Word to a whole new level!

- Use a concordance, lexicon, dictionary, and thesaurus to go deeper in your Quiet Time.

- Use the space provided in the margins to take notes, write down additional Scripture references you find, or to draw pictures that come to mind as you learn how to become "Anchored."

Anchored

Deep down you may have known, or at least hoped, there was more to life than what you saw with your physical eyes. Was Christianity only about dressing up for church on Sunday? I remember thinking something along those lines. "God, is this really all You are about? Is this all life is about: see how good you can go through the motions, and then you die?" I couldn't accept that what I saw was all there was, and I began to embark on a journey with God that changed my life. I was so fed up with the routines of the world and the rat race I lived in. I knew deep down I was created for more than the life I was living, and it had nothing to do with my social, ethnic, or economic status. I had been going through the motions of life, but not truly living.

We traveled, went on nice vacations, and we had lots of "stuff"—yet it was never enough. The person within me was never satisfied, so I kept striving, trying to curb the appetite. Nothing seemed to work—church wasn't helping, shopping wasn't helping, exercise wasn't helping, no achievements I made with my businesses were helping. I was fading out, not only from my marriage but my life as a whole, and I didn't even realize it. My tank was on "E," and no matter how hard I tried, I couldn't find the right fuel. I heard lies that whispered my young children really didn't need me and that my husband would be fine without me. I never contemplated suicide, but I now know many people who have while in this dark night of the soul.

My husband had started a Bible study called *Every Man A Warrior*, and I would come in at random times to see him studying Scripture or teaching our boys how to have a Quiet Time. It was bizarre, but I honestly thought the phase would pass, and we would go back to our dry, normal life, as usual. I was okay with that; at least it was predictable!

One evening, however, God showed me just how misinformed I had been. My husband came into the kitchen and asked if he could speak with me in the garage while he polished his car. Irritated that he wanted me to stop what I was doing to watch him rub on his car, I begrudgingly went. I sat on the steps with my face resting on a fist, aggravated, as my husband started to tell me a story. There was a man at work who had told him how his wife had left him. The conversation had already gone deeper than I expected, and my curiosity was piqued. I wondered out loud if she had cheated on him, to which my husband shared he had asked the man the same question. The man had replied, "No, there was no affair, but as I looked back over the last 20 years of our marriage, I could see that she was fading out of the picture, and I did nothing to fight for her." Adam and I were a decade into our marriage . . .

Adam then came over and knelt in front of me—car forgotten. He looked me in the eyes and said, "Jessie, I see you fading, and I'm going to fight for you! I'm not going to let you go!" I was stunned into silence. I would love to say that I cried and wrapped my arms around him, but I didn't. I was in a danger zone, and I had not even realized it. I hadn't seen the fade happening; I didn't realize how close I was to the edge. I had been staggering toward the slaughter, following an enemy made of lies. I wanted to believe, but the slow fade happens, well . . . slowly. No one had been investing in me; there was only the world of television and social media. My standards had plummeted, and my value had suddenly become based on what I could offer or accomplish. I was out of things to give. I didn't know how to make the Bible "work." It was as lifeless to me as my own heart.

I continued to watch my husband grow through his Quiet Times. He treated me differently. He became careful and tender with me, coaxing me out of my dark hole. Finally, one day, I came in to find Adam quizzing my kindergartner on his spelling words. Then Adam would be quizzed on his Scripture memory verses . . . by someone who couldn't read, mind you! As I stood there, soaking in what a godly leader looked like, I broke. I didn't know how to do what God was asking of me; I didn't know how to get back to good. Then God gave me a vision:

"... I saw a woman chasing her husband down a dusty gravel path in her makeshift armor made from scraps of wood and metal—she was ready for his every move. She knew all the ways he would wound her, and she was ready to take him out at the knees if necessary. A weapon in each hand, she stopped and saw him opposite her at the crossroad. He was no longer armed with the weapons of her destruction, like condescending looks and degrading comments.

He stood before her, bare-chested and empty-handed. He knew he had wounded her and misled her, so he stood before her willing to take whatever punishment she had come to dole out. The man had learned that it was his God-given design to bring his masculinity to her as a protective shield, rather than to control and manipulate her. Seeing he was unwilling to wound her, *the woman knew she had a choice to make. Her husband had walked into the design God laid out for him. Did she have the courage to do the same, to walk in the design God had created for her? Could she trust this new creation standing before her, that once forced her to build walls to protect the very heart she promised to his care? She knew he was not perfect and would still fail her at times. Was she willing to trust God with her wounded heart?*

With a deep breath from her lungs, she dropped the weapons at her feet and divested her makeshift armor. Underneath, her dress was dirty and tattered; her hair was unkempt. Her face was sweaty, smudged with dirt, and streaked with tears. She took a step forward, and as she placed her foot down, it landed on cool, clean white marble. Her hair was suddenly clean and brushed, her face radiant like the sun, and her dress was made of pure white linen as if spun from Heaven's loom. She placed her hand in the waiting palm of her husband, and together, side by side, they walked in the path the LORD prepared for them, to the treasure that awaited them both."

I was standing in my kitchen when God sent this vision to play across my mind. I had a choice to make, and in that moment, I couldn't get my armor off fast enough! All I had to do was take one baby step forward. I had stood on the sidelines carrying my burdens long enough. I had put all of my worth and value in my husband's hands, and in doing so, I set him up for failure!

He was never designed to be my everything, any more than I was designed to be his everything. That role had belonged and will always belong to Jesus. I had let his shortcomings and failures define my worth—a task that only God can fill. I decided to put the fate of my heart in my Heavenly Father's care.

The weight I had put on my marriage was too much for it to bear; the foundation was weak and crumbling. It was time to follow in my husband's footsteps and allow God to rewrite my heart. We both had our own journeys with God, but I had let Adam's journey define mine.

My burdens were too heavy, and I was tired. I couldn't do it anymore; I wanted freedom from the numbing rat race that had become my life. I went to Adam and asked him to show me how to have a Quiet Time. I wanted us to walk together in the path the LORD had laid for us. It was time for me to lay down my weapons and bust through the protective walls I had built around my heart.

As I began to journey with the Lord through His Word, it was as if I could look over and see Adam on his path, while I was on mine. Healing needed to happen individually before God could merge our paths and heal our marriage. He wanted to be sure we were both placing our confidence and identity in Him, and not one another. Through my time alone with God, He began to breathe life into the places in me that had long been dead. I discovered it to be an honor and a privilege to be a wife and mother. I found joy in laying my life down for my Bridegroom, my earthly husband, and my children. The Father taught me there was so much more to my life than the lies I had been feeding on. The proof of God's love for me was my very life—the fact that He had created me. He wanted me. He desired to know me, inside and out, and I realized I desired to know Him.

Since that time, my passion for God has not waned; it has only grown deeper and stronger, and my earthly marriage has become a reflection of that. Sometimes it is a constant battle to fight for Truth and stay anchored in what I have become convinced of through my explorations of God's heart. But the anchor is deep, and it always holds. Adam and I still face opposition, and I catch myself trying to make him an idol for my value and worth. However, I will not set him up for failure like that again; I respect him as a child of God and a man after God's heart. What a privilege it is to see him this way! I am no longer defined by his failures, for they are just as many as my own. I no longer "need" his constant attention and approval because I have the constant care and guidance of my LORD. I no longer fear where his thoughts are or if he will hurt me. I am finally able to realize that this is his journey with God alongside my own. And when he falls, it is an issue between him and God, not between him and me. However, I can be there to help him up!

Dear Sisters, this was the hardest leap of faith I ever made. I had to trust God with all my heart, all my soul, and all my mind (Matthew 22:36-38). God wasn't calling me to trust a man, but to trust God with my thoughts, feelings, safety, and security. This wasn't about me trusting my husband not to hurt me; this was about me trusting God to be faithful to me and never leave me—to learn to let God be my worth and value. I was in a marriage with another child of God who had his own spiritual journey.

YOU LEARN TO PUT YOUR IDENTITY IN JESUS BY PURPOSING TO GROW YOUR RELATIONSHIP WITH HIM—IT'S A CHOICE.

We had spent so many years pulling against one another instead of spurring the other on toward their true identity in Christ. All of a sudden, I realized this was a vertical issue between God and me, not a horizontal one between my husband and me.

I pray you seek the Lord for this same heart knowledge! I can paint the picture and give you the skills to make the leap and land well, but the leaping is up to you! Let me assure you that God is fully behind you, beneath you, above you, and ahead of you in this! If God is for you, then all you need to do is leap in faith!

Learning to Care for Your Spirit

DEUTERONOMY 8:1, 2-3, 6, 12-14 NIV84

¹Be careful to follow every command I am giving you today, so that you may live and increase . . . ²Remember how the Lord your God led you all the way in the desert . . . To humble you and to test you in order to know what was in your heart, whether or not you would keep his commands. ³He humbled you, causing you to hunger and then feeding you with manna, which neither you nor your fathers had known, to teach you that man does not live on bread alone but on every word that comes from the mouth of the lord . . . ⁶Observe the commands of the Lord your God walking in his ways and revering him . . . Be careful that you do not forget the Lord your God, failing to observe his commands, his laws, and his decrees that I am giving you this day. ¹²Otherwise, when you eat and are satisfied, when you build fine houses and settle down, ¹³and when your flocks grow large and your silver and gold increase and all you have is multiplied, ¹⁴then your heart will become proud and you will forget the lord your god who brought you out of Egypt, out of the land of slavery . . .

SPIRITUAL FOOD

Do you see? The flesh is fed with bread, but the Word of God feeds the spirit. There is so much more to this life than what meets the physical eye (2 Corinthians 4:18). In my story, I shared how I had starved my spirit, continually trying to fill the void with things of the world that were *supposed* to give me value, and how none of them worked (see Matthew 6:19-20). You were created by righteousness, and whether you accept it or not, you hunger for Him inside (Ephesians 2:14).

The Word of God was given to you for spiritual food; you were designed to hunger spiritually so that you would crave your Creator and seek His way. Through the Word, you learn His nature and character. You grow in your belief and allow His Spirit to work in you and through you for the glory of God, so that you can be a bright light in a dark world, manifesting God's glory in even greater ways than Jesus did while He was here on earth (John 14:12-14; John 21:25)!

Deuteronomy shows that God allows times in the desert to help you recognize the void in your heart that "things" cannot satisfy. The people of the Old Testament had the same issue as we do now—they were looking for physical satisfaction to fill the void in their hearts that only God can fill (see Deuteronomy 8:12). I'm not talking to the unsaved; I'm talking to the Church. Can you love God too much? Can you trust Him too much? Have any of us gotten close enough to find out? No, I don't think so. You can say I'm trying to over-spiritualize the Bible, but how does one over spiritualize The Spirit of God? Furthermore, we were made in His image (see Genesis 1:27).

JESUS, TEACH ME HOW TO DESIRE YOU MORE!

Why does all of this spiritual talk matter? You must understand that the Word was given to you to obey—not half-heartedly obey, but whole-heartedly obey! If God said it, there is a reason for it because He wastes nothing! In light of eternity, your life here on this earth is just a blip—a vapor (see James 4:14). Yet, what you do in that blip echoes forevermore. I do all this work in my heart, removing weeds of unrighteousness and infertile soil so I can be closer to the Father, now. As the Body, we must stop looking at the Word of God as a "good book." We must realize what it teaches, and the degree to which we apply the spiritual Truths to our own hearts determines how well we know the Father—which is the most important point (see Matthew 22:36-38)!

THEN JESUS WAS LED BY THE SPIRIT INTO THE WILDERNESS
TO BE TEMPTED THERE BY THE DEVIL. FOR FORTY DAYS AND
FORTY NIGHTS HE FASTED AND BECAME VERY HUNGRY.
DURING THAT TIME THE DEVIL CAME AND SAID TO HIM,
"IF YOU ARE THE SON OF GOD, TELL THESE STONES TO
BECOME LOAVES OF BREAD." BUT JESUS TOLD HIM,
"NO! THE SCRIPTURES SAY, 'PEOPLE DO NOT LIVE
BY BREAD ALONE, BUT BY EVERY WORD THAT
COMES FROM THE MOUTH OF GOD."
—MATTHEW 4:1-4 NLT

Just as Chandra in Lesson 6, "Forgiving Self" from Book 2, "Letting the Healer Heal" explained, she had held her inner man to the standards of the world, something she was not created to be. No matter how hard Chandra tried, she never measured up to what the world viewed as valuable and successful. This is because the world's value system is based on unrighteousness (see Matthew 6:19-20). It takes more effort to try to conform yourself to the way of the world than it does to the way of God because you were created in His image (see Genesis 1:27; Romans 8:31-32).

When you try to conform to the world, you are ineffectively trying to go against your God-given design, which explains why so many are utterly destitute inside (see Romans 8:2-9; John 14:17). I encourage you to pray the prayer of the father in Mark 9:24: "Lord I believe; help my unbelief!" There is more to you than you realize. God is way bigger than you have been taught (see John 21:25). This heart knowledge may uproot your life and change the direction you have been going with the choices you have been making regarding everything that pertains to you . . . like the men you have been pursuing or allowing to pursue you, career, habits, hobbies, and so on. On the other hand, you may discover you are right where you are supposed to be! Nonetheless, there is more to you than meets the eye (see 2 Corinthians 4:17-18). Walking In the New life is contingent upon how you feed your inner being. It's your choice—whether you feed her the deception of the world or the Truth of the Word (see Psalm 119:93).

FOR THIS REASON, I KNEEL BEFORE THE FATHER, FROM WHOM EVERY FAMILY IN HEAVEN AND ON EARTH DERIVES ITS NAME. I PRAY THAT OUT OF HIS GLORIOUS RICHES HE MAY STRENGTHEN YOU WITH POWER THROUGH HIS SPIRIT IN YOUR INNER BEING, SO THAT CHRIST MAY DWELL IN YOUR HEARTS THROUGH FAITH. AND I PRAY THAT YOU, BEING ROOTED AND ESTABLISHED IN LOVE, MAY HAVE POWER, TOGETHER WITH ALL THE LORD'S HOLY PEOPLE, TO GRASP HOW WIDE AND LONG AND HIGH AND DEEP IS THE LOVE OF CHRIST, AND TO KNOW THIS LOVE THAT SURPASSES KNOWLEDGE—THAT YOU MAY BE FILLED TO THE MEASURE OF ALL THE FULLNESS OF GOD.
—EPHESIANS 3:14-19 NIV

The Disciples and the Resurrection

I want to know Him when I see Him, like the women who were present at the Resurrection. I want to remember His words when I am faced with the unbelievable. When I hear things like, "Jesus loves you more than you could ever know," I do not want to doubt as the rest of the disciples did upon the news of Jesus's resurrection. Luke 24:11 states, "They did not believe the women because their words seemed to them like nonsense." Some of my words may seem like nonsense to you, but I encourage you to seek the Lord in prayer and through His Word. If I have interpreted the Word correctly, He will confirm it for you.

I WILL NEVER FORGET YOUR COMMANDS, BECAUSE THROUGH THEM YOU GAVE ME NEW LIFE.
—PSALM 119:93 ERV

The Battle

There is so much more to the Christian life than you can imagine (see John 21:25)! You'll have to trust what you have become convinced of about God's goodness and faithfulness to you through your Quiet Times to keep growing. This is the one thing the enemy doesn't want you to discover—who you were actually created to be! There is so much more for you, all you have to do is let your heart keep beating for Him! He will take it from there! The battle is a reality you see that is based on lies. These lies are not only about yourself but predominantly wrong doctrine and strongholds or mindsets about who God is and how far He will or will not go for you. This is the battle! Will you let the Word of God reign in your heart, soul, and mind? It is time to let it dwell in you richly. The Word is the final authority on anything that matters.

You must choose to earnestly put away the things which have tempered your thoughts, actions, words, and choices toward God and your identity in Him. The battle is deception—smoke and mirrors. All you have to do to win is keep your eyes fixed on Jesus. You do not have to stay in a place of defeat, that is not what God wants for you. But you do have to choose Truth in the moment! Then, you will discover what this life is truly about!

If you are too weak to stand, lift your eyes to heaven and make your heart available to the One who created you. You may be face down on the battlefield with a knife stuck in your back, but remember, God doesn't need your strength—He REIGNS in your weakness! He will come for you and be your Defender. All you have to do is surrender the fight to Him! You can do this!

When it comes to His beloved children, our Father will move heaven and earth to reach us (see Psalm 18:1-19; John 21:25; Mark 7:13). It is not up to us to dictate what God can and cannot do or will and will not do in His sovereignty. We honestly do not know enough of His Word to make such bold statements. Ask God to reveal the ways you have limited Him from being glorified in your life. Spend at least 30 minutes listening in silence, then write down anything you feel you heard.

Ask His forgiveness for anything that was revealed during the listening prayer time on the previous page.

The Battle Strategy

HOW TO SELECT YOUR VERSE

The Word of God is your battle strategy. It instructs you on how to win the battles you face every day in a fallen world. Scripture has an answer for every situation. Whether it is an attack of the enemy or results of bad choices, the Bible has a solution for it.

This exercise is to help you continue growing stronger as a woman of the Word by customizing your weapons of war!

HERE'S THE PLAN:

1. Using the skills from Book 2, "Letting the Healer Heal," identify the lie and flip it for truth. God will most often reveal a heart condition in you that needs surrendering! This is the next step in building on Hurt Letters and purifying your soul. Please don't forget these two things:

   - The world is full of hurting people, so don't assume you will outgrow Hurt Letters.

   - You will never outgrow the need for repentance and forgiveness this side of heaven.

2. Once you have identified a lie, then identify any sins that may be a result of the lie.

   - Examples: If you were struggling with self-worth, then you may have given into seeking approval from man. If you gave in to fear and doubt, then you may have given in to not trusting God for your safety and security, etc. These are all examples of sin that wounds can cause. When we seek our identity in God, we don't have self-worth issues.

- Often our issues with people are actually a reflection of our insecurities with God the Father.

3. Flip the lie for truth. If you are feeling worthless, what does God say about you?

4. Next, find a verse that anchors the truth you found when you flipped the lie.

- For example, search the Internet for, "Scripture that has to do with God's love for me," or whatever your present battle is. Be sure to start your search with the word "Scripture."

5. Pick the verse that speaks most to your battle. This verse becomes your new memory verse—your customized battle strategy!

6. Whenever you hear the lie, draw your customized sword that was made just for your hand and recite the verse out loud until truth wins!

7. This is a choice! No one can choose this for you! If you want to win, go to the Word and do what's right. Fight for the woman on the inside, the one for whom Jesus gave His life!

REMEMBER:

1. This is your very life! The woman inside you is worth fighting for! She was created and is cherished by God! Don't neglect her!

2. Once you get set free, you must choose to stay free. Remember the power of choice.

3. Remember what you have become convinced of and who taught it to you (see 2 Timothy 3:14).

- Review your Quiet Times often. God has me "remember" our times together and all the things He has taught me. Sometimes the lessons you have learned get pushed to the back of your memory as you are learning new ones.

- This is one of the main reasons why written Quiet Times are so important. When we record our journey with God in writing, we can review where we have been and remember where we are going.

4. Run to God instead of your old default mode.

    - When you feel yourself doubting, and things start to feel off in your spirit, stop and seek the Lord. Ask the Lord to reveal whatever it is in you that is off and not of Him. Listen with ears to hear; look with eyes to see.

    - Be sure to quiet your soul and give yourself time to hear. This more than likely won't work in a car full of kids or while your attention is divided. If He matters to you, take the time to become fully present to Him.

    - Keep seeking until you identify the problem. This is a gentle reminder that if you don't hear clearly, the issue is on your end, not His (see Isaiah 59:1-2). Remember, these things take time.

5. Choose to be pure of heart and purposefully tear down strongholds and idols that try to take God's place in your heart and mind.

6. Yield to God's Word, especially when it is hard! You will not be doing any of this in your own strength but in His. All you have to do is lift your eyes to His and keep them there (see Hebrews 12:2)!

It's Past Time to Get Serious

JAMES 4:1-10 MSG

[1-2] Where do you think all these appalling wars and quarrels come from? Do you think they just happen? Think again. They come about because you want your own way, and fight for it deep inside yourselves. You lust for what you don't have and are willing to kill to get it. You want what isn't yours and will risk violence to get your hands on it.

[2-3] You wouldn't think of just asking God for it, would you? And why not? Because you know you'd be asking for what you have no right to. You're spoiled children, each wanting your own way.

⁴⁻⁶ You're cheating on God. If all you want is your own way, flirting with the world every chance you get, you end up enemies of God and his way. And do you suppose God doesn't care? The proverb has it that "he's a fiercely jealous lover." And what he gives in love is far better than anything else you'll find. It's common knowledge that "God goes against the willful proud; God gives grace to the willing humble."

⁷⁻¹⁰ So let God work his will in you. Yell a loud no to the Devil and watch him scamper. Say a quiet yes to God and he'll be there in no time. Quit dabbling in sin. Purify your inner life. Quit playing the field. Hit bottom, and cry your eyes out. The fun and games are over. Get serious, really serious. Get down on your knees before the Master; it's the only way you'll get on your feet.

 ## Review

1. You will never outgrow the Healer . . . ever!

2. You will never outgrow your need for repentance and forgiveness.

3. Choosing Truth over lies for your battle strategy is a choice you get to make. Choose wisely!

 ## Main Take-Away

What was your main take-away from this lesson?

 ## Before Your Next Meeting

1. Try to have a Quiet Time at least four times this week using the verses listed for Lesson 8.

2. Memorize **Hebrews 10:23-25** this week.

Notes

Notes

Sustaining Through Seasons

KEY POINT

Learn how to stay faithful to Jesus and maintain spiritual growth through the wrestles of life.

WHY THIS MATTERS

When you learn how not to lose hope in Jesus when disappointment comes, you begin to win the battles and walk in the Spirit.

HOW TO APPLY

Part of sustaining is identifying the warning signs God sends when you are headed off course. You stay faithful in hard seasons when you remember the skills you have learned and why they are so important—intimacy with Jesus.

LESSON 8

Sustaining Through Seasons

MEMORY VERSES

Hebrews 10:23-25 (Write your memory verse in the space below.)

QUIET TIME VERSES

Hebrews 10:1-39; Galatians 5:16-26; Psalm 42:1-11; Galatians 6:9-10; 2 Timothy 3:10-17; Isaiah 66:9; 1 Corinthians 15:33-34

Complete Lesson 8 and try to have four to seven Quiet Times before your next meeting. To ensure you are using the verse in the correct context, be sure to read several verses before and after the suggested Quiet Time passage(s).

KEY POINT

Learn how to stay faithful to Jesus and maintain spiritual growth through the wrestles of life.

WHY THIS MATTERS

When you learn how not to lose hope in Jesus when disappointment comes, you begin to win the battles and walk in the Spirit.

HOW TO APPLY

Part of sustaining is identifying the warning signs God sends when you are headed off course. You stay faithful in hard seasons when you remember the skills you have learned and why they are so important—this is intimacy with Jesus.

Leader's Notes

- This lesson may take more than one or two weeks. If a group member has to miss causing the group to sit longer than two weeks in a lesson, find a time to meet with her one-on-one or over the phone so the group can keep moving forward.

- PRAY for your group to remain faithful to God in dry seasons.

- Highlight one or two questions from the lesson to be discussed in group time, allowing each person to share an answer. For quick reference, write the page numbers of the questions you chose to discuss below.

Navigating Your Group Time

- Spend 15-20 minutes in worship.

- As the time of worship comes to a close, the leader should begin the WAR method of prayer.

- Write a quick summary of Lesson 8 in the space below. Share this with the group to begin the lesson after the time of prayer is finished

- Have group members share their "Main Take-Away" from the end of the lesson.

- Have each person share a Quiet Time.

- If time allows, have each person share an answer from the questions the leader highlighted (1-2 questions).

- Read sections: "Review" and "Before Your Next Lesson".

- Break into pairs and recite your verses.

- Remind everyone to sign off on each other's course record in the back of the book.

LESSON 8

Sustaining Through Seasons

MEMORY VERSES

Hebrews 10:23-25 (Write your memory verse in the space below.)

QUIET TIME VERSES

Hebrews 10:1-39; Galatians 5:16-26; Psalm 42:1-11; Galatians 6:9-10; 2 Timothy 3:10-17; Isaiah 66:9; 1 Corinthians 15:33-34

Complete Lesson 8 and try to have four to seven Quiet Times before your next meeting. To ensure you are using the verse in the correct context, be sure to read several verses before and after the suggested Quiet Time passage(s).

KEY POINT

Knowing how to stay faithful to Jesus and maintain spiritual growth through the wrestles of life.

WHY THIS MATTERS

When you learn how not to lose hope in Jesus when disappointment comes, you begin to win the battles and walk in the Spirit.

HOW TO APPLY

Part of sustaining is identifying the warning signs God sends when you are headed off course. You stay faithful in hard seasons when you remember the skills you have learned and why they are so important—this is intimacy with Jesus.

Participant's Notes

- Complete this lesson before your next meeting. Be sure to answer the questions marked with a discussion bubble and be ready to share your answers with the group. It's important to remember there are no wrong answers to the questions throughout the lessons because they are your thoughts, so be free in how you answer!

- PRAY for your group to have faith to remain faithful to God in dry seasons.

- Use a concordance, lexicon, dictionary, and thesaurus to go deeper in your Quiet Time.

- Use the space provided in the margins to take notes, write down additional Scripture references you find, or to draw pictures that come to mind as you become equipped in "Sustaining Thru the Seasons."

Sustaining Through Seasons

**. . . I WILL NOT CAUSE PAIN WITHOUT ALLOWING SOMETHING
NEW TO BE BORN, SAYS THE LORD.
—ISAIAH 66:9 NCV**

It had been months since beginning her journey of growing closer to Jesus, and Sandy had not struggled with thoughts of suicide since. She had been going strong for a while and felt like nothing could bring her down! Her Quiet Times had been consistent and meaningful, with few days missed. Sandy's *Cultivating Holy Beauty* group loved getting daily encouragement from her through the group text.

Due to summer schedule conflicts, the group needed to take a short break. Sandy wasn't worried about the time away from her group since she had been so consistent in her time alone with God. She felt confident and planned to keep the group text going strong with daily, encouraging nuggets from her Quiet Time. However, after the first week of not meeting, it was like she hit a wall! She couldn't seem to find the zeal for purposing her time alone with God. Sandy persevered at first, but she found no nuggets of truth in her Quiet Time, and it just felt forced.

Finally, one day she decided to stop persevering, thinking a little break would help. Sandy promised herself she would find another way to spend time with God and skipped her morning Quiet Time, going about her day. Before she knew it, days had passed before Sandy had purposed to seek God through a Quiet Time and prayer. As the days ticked by, more guilt and shame weighed on her. Sandy began to isolate herself and quit sending encouraging texts to the group, confident of their disappointment in her.

One day, out of nowhere, she heard the sneaky old lie again, "Everyone would be better off if you weren't here, ya know? You are such a disappointment. You are always letting everyone down, aren't you?!" Sandy was shocked at the thought! It had been so long since she heard those thoughts, and it caught her completely off guard. "No one even noticed you stopped sending those texts; they are all probably glad you quit blowing their phones up every morning!"

Sandy began to cry as she agreed with the thought that everyone would, in fact, be better off without her. Depression seemed to walk right in the front door, kicking his feet up and getting comfortable in her mind. In a moment, it seemed all the progress she had made was gone, as if it were all a farce! She began to contemplate suicide again as despair tried to shoot its deep roots into the soil of her heart. However, there was something very different about that soil now. It was not as receptive to that sickly little seed as it once was. The truth in her heart sprang into action as it identified an intruder! As this awareness reached Sandy, she realized she knew exactly how to fight this battle and persevere. Sandy remembered the Scripture she had memorized for such a time as this. As she recited, "*Finally, brothers and sisters, whatever is true, whatever is noble, whatever is right, whatever is pure, whatever is lovely, whatever is admirable—if anything is excellent or praiseworthy—think about such things*" (Philippians 4:8 NIV), she envisioned her hands closing around that little prickly root and yanking it up! Suddenly, she was overwhelmed with the mercy and graciousness of God! She had done nothing to deserve that kind of life raft, yet the Father still plunged His hand in after her as He stood on top of the water seeing her sinking!

The look on His face wasn't worried about her safety or angry that she had forgotten so quickly. It was confident and caring. In the midst of the battle, she had remembered and frantically sought His gaze again. He was easy to find because she knew Him so well. Sandy's eyes locked with His as songs of praise and worship came from her lips. By becoming a woman of faith in who God is, Sandy had been victorious in her battle!

Sustaining When It's Hard

2 TIMOTHY 3:10-17 NIV84

[10] You, however, know all about my teaching, my way of life, my purpose, faith, patience, love, endurance, [11] persecutions, sufferings—what kinds of things happened to me… the persecutions I endured. Yet the Lord rescued me from all of them. [12] In fact, everyone who wants to live a godly life in Christ Jesus will be persecuted, [13] while evil men and imposters will go from bad to worse, deceiving and being deceived. [14] But as for you, continue in what you have learned and have become convinced of, because you know those from whom you learned it, [15] and how from infancy you have known the Holy Scriptures, which are able

to make you wise for salvation through faith in Christ Jesus. [16] All scripture is God-breathed and is useful for teaching, rebuking, correcting and training in righteousness, [17] so that the man of God may be thoroughly equipped for every good work.

CONTINUING TO GROW

In the passage from 2 Timothy, Paul tells Timothy, his disciple, how to carry on in this new way of life. Continue doing the things that led you to this freedom in the first place: Stay in the Word, as it will point you to all things that are good! Quiet Times, meditating, and memorizing Scripture, praying the WAR method of prayer, writing Hurt Letters, and listening for Love Letters are all weapons to fight against the oppression of the world. God's Word is like a soothing balm to our wounds.

Spending time in Scripture every day is essential for your journey ahead. Though you may not be spiritually anemic anymore, there will always be new spiritual truth from God's Word that needs to be planted in your heart as God's Spirit continues to bring you back to life. This is how we sustain our relationship with God; you never have to worry about growing stagnant in your walk with God if you are seeking Him daily (see Matthew 7:7-8 NIV). You only fail if you quit!

DRY SPELLS

I often hear of women fearing they will lose this deep connection with God after the curriculum is over. However, spiritually maturing never has to stop! As you begin to lead groups of women through *Cultivating Holy Beauty*, you will pass on the spiritual truths that transformed your heart. Your life will have new purpose— kingdom purpose! God will continue to refine and grow you on deeper levels as the beauty of spiritual maturity is carried forward when you begin discipling others. Spiritual growth does not stop this side of heaven! There is intimacy with Jesus, and then there is intimacy with Jesus—there is no next best thing!

WE MUST HOLD TIGHTLY TO THE HOPE THAT WE SAY IS OURS. AFTER ALL, WE CAN TRUST THE ONE WHO MADE THE AGREEMENT WITH US. WE SHOULD KEEP ON ENCOURAGING EACH OTHER TO BE THOUGHTFUL AND TO DO HELPFUL THINGS. SOME PEOPLE HAVE GOTTEN OUT OF THE HABIT OF MEETING FOR WORSHIP, BUT WE MUST NOT DO THAT. WE SHOULD KEEP ON ENCOURAGING EACH OTHER, ESPECIALLY SINCE YOU KNOW THAT THE DAY OF THE LORD'S COMING IS GETTING CLOSER.
—HEBREWS 10:23-25 CEV

An essential element in pushing through dry spells is surrounding yourself with a godly community. It's one thing to be a light for the lost and hurting, but it's altogether different whom you confide in when you are struggling and in need of right and wise counsel! My family has made a point to meet with a few other families, usually on Friday nights, solely to worship and pray. The kids join in as we sing our favorite songs to the Lord. We end the night by sharing what God has been teaching us and praying as His Spirit speaks to our hearts. It's rich and edifying! The purpose of these nights is only to exalt the Lord, being sure to keep Him the center of our worship and conversation.

God is patient and kind, going to whatever lengths necessary to reveal the things in you that keep you apart from Him. He loves you that much! Romans 7:14 says that sin makes you unspiritual. When I learned this, it made me pause and wonder about my own dry spells in the past and if they may be linked to hidden sin. I believe this is why God allows the awareness of that distance at times; it's a wake-up call for the ones who care. It drives us back to Him.

1 John 1:8 states, "If we claim to be without sin, we deceive ourselves, and the truth is not in us." With that being said, you cannot ever assume that the problem is God. The problem always lies in your humanness. God says He will never forsake you, but you can and do turn away from God when you choose sin (see Matthew 28:20). Every time you give in to the sinful nature of your flesh, you are ultimately turning your back on God. He doesn't want to leave you vulnerable any

more than you would want to leave your own child vulnerable to an enemy. He knows you need Him close!

BE ANGRY AND DO NOT SIN. MEDITATE WITHIN YOUR HEART ON YOUR BED, AND BE STILL.
—PSALM 4:4 NKJV

Let me reiterate: If you feel distant from God, it's not His problem—it's yours. These are hard and straightforward words, but it's time you and I start eating from the Word like spiritual adults. Don't you want that? If you are feeling distant from God, I suggest you use the skills you learned in Book 2 and talk to Him about it. Seek Him for the purpose and/or cause!

When we sin, He doesn't go off and sulk with hurt feelings. His heart breaks for us because He knows we have turned toward the darkness instead of the Light, and that only brings us more pain. He can handle whatever it is you are struggling with. Just as you learned in Book 2 "Letting the Healer Heal," God is not overwhelmed by your sin, and He isn't threatened by whatever unbelief you have where He is concerned. He's still the God of miracles, whether you and I believe it or not. He is still the God of Creation, whether Creation believes it or not. He is secure in His Godhood, and He can and will handle whatever questions, doubt, unbelief, anger, or sin you have in your heart if you allow Him access. Again—this is your choice.

WHEN YOU FAIL, EXPECT TO SEE MY FACE—NOT MY BACK.
—ABBA

1 CORINTHIANS 10:1-13 NIV

[1]For I do not want you to be ignorant of the fact, brothers and sisters, that our ancestors were all under the cloud and that they all passed through the sea. [2] They were all baptized into Moses in the cloud and in the sea. [3] They all ate the same spiritual food [4] and drank the same spiritual drink; for they drank from the spiritual rock that accompanied them, and that rock was Christ. [5] Nevertheless, God was not pleased with most of them; their bodies were scattered in the wilderness.

⁶ Now these things occurred as examples to keep us from setting our hearts on evil things as they did. ⁷ Do not be idolaters, as some of them were; as it is written: "the people sat down to eat and drink and got up to indulge in revelry." ⁸ We should not commit sexual immorality, as some of them did—and in one day twenty-three thousand of them died. ⁹ We should not test Christ, as some of them did—and were killed by snakes. ¹⁰ And do not grumble, as some of them did—and were killed by the destroying angel.

¹¹ These things happened to them as examples and were written down as warnings for us, on whom the culmination of the ages has come. ¹² So, if you think you are standing firm, be careful that you don't fall! ¹³No temptation has overtaken you except what is common to mankind. And God is faithful; He will not let you be tempted beyond what you can bear. But when you are tempted, He will also provide a way out so that you can endure it.

BELIEVING THROUGH DOUBT

Answers to our modern-day problems can always be found in history. Everything you need to know about how to sustain your relationship with God throughout the different seasons of life can be found in Scripture. I am so thankful for God's Word!

Imagine what it would have been like to walk through the parted Red Sea or to talk with Jesus and actually see Him heal the sick, restore sight to the blind, and raise the dead to life! Talk about a mountaintop moment! And we think hearing Love Letters from God is a big deal . . . well, actually, it is! However, what about after Jesus had gone back to the Father and He wasn't right in front of them? When all hope seemed lost and the disciples felt alone—what then? Scripture says even after Jesus revealed Himself to them, "some doubted" (see Matthew 28:17).

Just like Peter, I want to say, "No! Not me, Lord!" But sadly, the truth is, yes—me. Sometimes it feels like my faith is so slippery that I cannot hold on to it in the face of my battles. You will have these moments—stay faithful! There will be mountaintop moments or days, when you feel your faith could move mountains! However, the day-to-day stuff isn't lived just on the mountaintops; it is often lived in the valleys—where the wrestle takes place. This is how we survive the day-to-day, by going to God and doing what's right over and over again, not just when it is hard, but especially when it is hard!

What are the critical factors listed in 1 Corinthians 10:1-13 on pages 145-146, that caused the Israelites to fall? List three:

There will be times when your time alone with God feels forced or dry, and it is the last thing you want to do! Doesn't marriage sometimes feel that way? What is the first thing you should do in this moment? (Hint: see 2 Timothy 3:14; Hebrews 10:23-25.)

Warning Signs

Usually, multiple warning signs crop up when you start walking in your own strength and relying less on God, just as we saw with Eve in Genesis 3. Upon deeper investigation of Matthew 26:31-75, I discovered a common theme between the accounts of the fall of Peter and Eve. For Peter, it began in Matthew 26:31. Jesus prophesied that Peter would fall away, but Peter didn't believe Him. Peter's first mistake was he despised prophecy and rejected the Word. He did not believe what Jesus told him (see John 1:14).

The second thing that led to Peter's fall was his confidence in his own strength. Matthew 26:35 records Peter saying, "even if I have to die with you, I will never disown you." Peter did not expect to deny Jesus and underestimated his own weakness. This is true for all of us when our Quiet Times are going strong, and our cup is overflowing. It is easy to get overconfident, thinking it will always feel this way—until the going gets tough and your cup seems to be dry and thirsty!

Thirdly, Peter failed to pray. Jesus called Peter out in Matthew 26:40 when he said, "So you could not keep watch with Me one hour?" Matthew 26:51 tells of a crowd that came looking for Jesus armed with swords and clubs. Once Judas identified Jesus with the kiss, the crowd came and laid hands on Jesus. John 18:10 clarifies that Peter drew his sword and cut off the ear of the high priest's servant. This leads me to the fourth point: Peter gave in to his carnality, agreed with the world, and acted out of his flesh when he drew his sword and cut off Malchus' ear. This is also another instance of Peter standing in his own strength and going ahead of God.

Fifth, Peter forgot that God is all-powerful. In verse 53 Jesus says, "Do you think that I cannot now pray to My Father, and He will at once give Me more than twelve legions of angels?" Peter was so focused on the crowd that he lost sight of his faith. Forgetting that God was in control, he took matters into his own hands. It's interesting, isn't it? Previously, Peter sank in the water when he took his focus off Jesus and focused on his surroundings (see Matthew 14:30).

The sixth thing that led to Peter's fall was that he distanced himself from Jesus. "Peter followed Him at a distance . . . " (Matthew 26:58 NIV). You will see this happen when you start skipping Quiet Times. When you "just aren't feeling it," persevere and keep pushing through! This is a mature move. Sometimes I don't want to have a written Quiet Time, so I will just quiet myself before Him. I am careful to make myself present before the Lord daily, regardless of what it looks like. You won't regret it! Lastly, Peter denied truth again when he identified himself with the enemy by "calling down curses on himself" (Matthew 26:74). When he heard the rooster crow, he remembered what Jesus had said, and he "went outside and wept bitterly" (Matthew 26:75).

Many times I've realized that I've fallen short and have not glorified God. I want to be a pure vessel for the Lord. I want Him to be able to inhabit every ounce of my being. However, I so often fall short. God doesn't call us to be perfect; He calls us to have an open heart toward Him, to be repentant, and learn from our mistakes. I can't be perfect, but I can be repentant. By keeping my heart, eyes, and ears tuned to the Lord and no one else, I can expect to keep a sin inventory of no more than one. Meaning, when I sin, I become instantly aware of it because of my closeness to the Father, allowing His Holy Spirit to convict me with His still small voice, leading me to repent and turn from my sin.

RECAP OF WARNING SIGNS FROM PETER'S EXPERIENCE:

1. Never reject the Word or doubt that it applies to you. Keep reading! (See Proverbs 30:5).

2. Do not stand in your own strength (see 2 Corinthians 12:9).

3. Do not fail to pray (see 1 Thessalonians 5:17).

4. Be a woman of the Word, not a woman of the world. Do not let your flesh rule you (see 1 John 5:19).

5. Do not forget the power of God! He desires your obedience, not your help (see Jeremiah 17:7).

6. Do not allow yourself to be isolated from Jesus (see James 4:8).

7. Claim truth and don't agree with the lies of the enemy (see John 8:44)!

There will be times when it feels like you have no one—no matter how hard you try to reach out to other Christians around you, no one responds. Do not let these moments define you! Remember what you have become convinced of and Who taught it to you (see 2 Timothy 3:14)! Keep your eyes on Him! He's the only One who can save you. At the end of the day, it's about you and Jesus. While community is vital, it's not your lifeline—Jesus is!

"How to Sustain" Exercise:

LEARNING YOUR WARNING SIGNS

Warning signs may look a little different for each of us. Apply the instructions from "Recap of Warning Signs from Peter's Experience" to your life. For each question below, list at least one example of how each warning sign manifests itself in your daily life. How do these lead to a downfall of your own? Do you see a pattern?

> Ask the Holy Spirit to show you any doubt you may have about the Word, along with warning signs that could potentially lead you off course. Be sure to come back and list anything the Spirit reveals to you.

Was there a time you stood in your own strength or sought vindication for yourself, not allowing God to be your Defender?

List an instance that would have turned out so much better if you had remembered to pray:

Was there a temptation that you gave in to, letting your flesh rule when you knew it mattered to God that you refrain (language, lust, gossip, lack of self-control, etc.,)?

Give an example of how you didn't trust in the power of God.

Was there a time when you allowed yourself to be isolated from God or a godly community?

Can you recall a time in the past week where you agreed with a lie of the enemy and did not claim truth or ask for forgiveness for coming into agreement with the lie?

Review

1. Remember what you have become convinced of and Who taught it to you (see 2 Timothy 3:14)!

2. Romans 7:14 says sin makes us unspiritual. If you are feeling distant from God, talk to Him about it and ask Him to show you what is going on.

3. Surrounding yourself with people who are turning away from the desires of the world and seeking Jesus is vital (see 1 Corinthians 15:33)!

Main Take-Away

What was your main take-away from this lesson?

Notes

Notes

Appendix

Book 3: Walking In the New
COURSE REQUIREMENTS

LESSON TITLE	MEMORY VERSES	LEADER INITIAL - DATE
Lesson 1: Walking In the New	_____	_____
Lesson 2: Justified	_____	_____
Lesson 3: Surrendered	_____	_____
Lesson 4: Choosing What You Value	_____	_____
Lesson 5: My Everything	_____	_____
Lesson 6: A Woman After God's Own Heart	_____	_____
Lesson 7: Anchored	_____	_____
Lesson 8: Sustaining Thru Seasons	_____	_____

FINAL RECORDS FOR BOOK 3

Finish All Eight Lessons	_____
Memorize Eight Scripture Passages	_____
Total Number of Quiet Times I've Completed	_____

About the Author

Like many of Jesus' first disciples, I did not come into ministry with theological training or the eloquence of someone who had been taught in church from an early age. A series of hard life choices and the consequences that followed left gaping wounds in my life, exposing a heart that was spiritually dying and in desperate need of a Savior. And this is where Jesus closed the divide, drawing me to Himself through a series of dreams and revealing His plan of salvation to me. I found myself humbled, bent low at the foot of the cross. I stand victorious today only because of Jesus.

In 2013, my husband, Adam, began the ***Every Man a Warrior*** discipleship program by Lonnie Berger. It was through Christ's transformative overflow in my husband's life that God awakened me. He called me to begin writing ***Cultivating Holy Beauty*** upon realizing that lies had held me captive for over a decade *after* my salvation. As I grew in my heart knowledge of the Word, I became convinced of Proverbs 30:5, "Every word of God is flawless." Then one day, it clicked: "All of God's promises are true, and they are for me!" In that moment, my heart became like a bright city on a hillside. It was as if a light had been turned on inside me, and others wanted to know what had changed! I was being presented with one opportunity after another to share the Gospel—drawing back a shade to awaken the Bride of Christ to a Son that's already risen!

As one of His commissioned disciples, I am deeply committed to preparing the Bride for His return. I don't have an impressive résumé. I'm not rehearsed in the art of storytelling or teaching Bible studies. My only qualifier is Jesus. I am His humble servant and instrument. These words are an overflow of His work in *my* life. You can't fall in love with the Creator of the universe and keep silent! His love changes everything. I want you to *know* Him. Will you arise and join me in pursuing Him? He wants to be found (Jeremiah 29:13).

Jessie North

Daughter of the Living God, Wife, and Mother
AUTHOR
Cultivating Holy Beauty

The Quiet Time Worksheet

Cultivating Holy Beauty

KEY POINT:

FAVORITE VERSE:

REWRITE THE VERSE:

In your own words and without changing the meaning

APPLICATION & PRAYER

HOW might this verse change the way you live? WHY does practicing this truth in your daily walk with God matter? Write a PRAYER to the Lord sharing what you learned and what the verse means to you.

EMPHASIZE:

Focus on different words to better understand their context and meaning.

ASK QUESTIONS:

IS THERE...

A PROMISE TO CLAIM?

A SIN TO AVOID?

A COMMAND TO OBEY?

SOMETHING NEW YOU LEARNED ABOUT GOD?

The Quiet Time Worksheet

CULTIVATING
Holy Beauty

KEY POINT:

FAVORITE VERSE:

REWRITE THE VERSE:
In your own words and without changing the meaning

APPLICATION & PRAYER
HOW might this verse change the way you live? WHY does practicing this truth in your daily walk with God matter? Write a PRAYER to the Lord sharing what you learned and what the verse means to you.

EMPHASIZE:
Focus on different words to better understand their context and meaning.

ASK QUESTIONS:

IS THERE...

A PROMISE TO CLAIM?

A SIN TO AVOID?

A COMMAND TO OBEY?

SOMETHING NEW YOU LEARNED ABOUT GOD?

The Quiet Time Worksheet

CULTIVATING
Holy Beauty

KEY POINT:

FAVORITE VERSE:

REWRITE THE VERSE:
In your own words and without changing the meaning

APPLICATION & PRAYER
HOW might this verse change the way you live? WHY does practicing this truth in your daily walk with God matter? Write a PRAYER to the Lord sharing what you learned and what the verse means to you.

EMPHASIZE:
Focus on different words to better understand their context and meaning.

ASK QUESTIONS:

IS THERE...

A PROMISE TO CLAIM?

A SIN TO AVOID?

A COMMAND TO OBEY?

SOMETHING NEW YOU LEARNED ABOUT GOD?

The Quiet Time Worksheet

KEY POINT:

FAVORITE VERSE:

REWRITE THE VERSE:

In your own words and without changing the meaning

APPLICATION & PRAYER

HOW might this verse change the way you live? WHY does practicing this truth in your daily walk with God matter? Write a PRAYER to the Lord sharing what you learned and what the verse means to you.

EMPHASIZE:

Focus on different words to better understand their context and meaning.

ASK QUESTIONS:

IS THERE...

A PROMISE TO CLAIM?

A SIN TO AVOID?

A COMMAND TO OBEY?

SOMETHING NEW YOU LEARNED ABOUT GOD?

CULTIVATING
Holy Beauty

The Quiet Time Worksheet

KEY POINT:

FAVORITE VERSE:

REWRITE THE VERSE:

In your own words and without changing the meaning

APPLICATION & PRAYER

HOW might this verse change the way you live? WHY does practicing this truth in your daily walk with God matter? Write a PRAYER to the Lord sharing what you learned and what the verse means to you.

EMPHASIZE:

Focus on different words to better understand their context and meaning.

ASK QUESTIONS:

IS THERE...

A PROMISE TO CLAIM?

A SIN TO AVOID?

A COMMAND TO OBEY?

SOMETHING NEW YOU LEARNED ABOUT GOD?

The Quiet Time Worksheet

CULTIVATING
Holy Beauty

KEY POINT:

FAVORITE VERSE:

REWRITE THE VERSE:

In your own words and without changing the meaning

APPLICATION & PRAYER

HOW might this verse change the way you live? WHY does practicing this truth in your daily walk with God matter? Write a **PRAYER** to the Lord sharing what you learned and what the verse means to you.

EMPHASIZE:

Focus on different words to better understand their context and meaning.

ASK QUESTIONS:

IS THERE...

A PROMISE TO CLAIM?

A SIN TO AVOID?

A COMMAND TO OBEY?

SOMETHING NEW YOU LEARNED ABOUT GOD?

2 Corinthians 5:17

Romans 5:1-2

Galatians 1:10

Romans 12:2

CHAPTER 1: WALKING IN THE NEW (W.I.N.)

CHAPTER 2: JUSTIFIED

BOOK 3: WALKING IN THE NEW

Scripture Memory

BOOK 3: WALKING IN THE NEW

Scripture Memory

CHAPTER 3: SURRENDERED

CHAPTER 4: CHOOSING WHAT YOU VALUE

BOOK 3: WALKING IN THE NEW

Scripture Memory

BOOK 3: WALKING IN THE NEW

Scripture Memory

BOOK 3: WALKING IN THE NEW

Ephesians 4:1-3

BOOK 3: WALKING IN THE NEW

CHAPTER 5: MY EVERYTHING

John 15:9-10

CHAPTER 6: A WOMAN AFTER GOD'S OWN HEART

BOOK 3: WALKING IN THE NEW

James 1:22

BOOK 3: WALKING IN THE NEW

CHAPTER 7: ANCHORED

Hebrews 10:23-25

CHAPTER 8: SUSTAINING THRU SEASONS

CHAPTER 5: MY EVERYTHING

CHAPTER 6: A WOMAN AFTER GOD'S OWN HEART

BOOK 3: WALKING IN THE NEW
Scripture Memory

BOOK 3: WALKING IN THE NEW
Scripture Memory

CHAPTER 7: ANCHORED

CHAPTER 8: SUSTAINING THRU SEASONS

BOOK 3: WALKING IN THE NEW
Scripture Memory

BOOK 3: WALKING IN THE NEW
Scripture Memory

BOOK 3: WALKING IN THE NEW

BOOK 3: WALKING IN THE NEW

BOOK 3: WALKING IN THE NEW

BOOK 3: WALKING IN THE NEW

BOOK 3: WALKING IN THE NEW

Scripture Memory

BOOK 3: WALKING IN THE NEW

Scripture Memory

BOOK 3: WALKING IN THE NEW

Scripture Memory

BOOK 3: WALKING IN THE NEW

Scripture Memory

CULTIVATING
Holy Beauty

Women's Authentic Discipleship
It's That Simple!

Please Share Your Journey With Us!

I believe movements of God fly on the wings of testimonies! We would love to hear how Cultivating Holy Beauty has helped grow your walk with God!

www.CultivatingHolyBeauty.com/yourjourney

Notes